Geraldene Holt's
Travelling
Food

By the same author

GERALDENE HOLT'S CAKE STALL

Geraldene Holt's
Travelling Food

A practical guide to over 200 movable feasts

Illustrations by Prue Theobalds

HODDER AND STOUGHTON
LONDON SYDNEY AUCKLAND TORONTO

British Library Cataloguing in Publication Data
Holt, Geraldene
    Geraldene Holt's travelling food.
    1. Cookery
    I. Title
    641.57   TX652

    ISBN 0 340 27836 6

Hodder and Stoughton Editorial Office: 47 Bedford Square, London WC1B 3DP.

For Alexander and Madeleine, with love

ACKNOWLEDGEMENTS

I am grateful to many members of my family and to a host of friends for advice and help in writing this book. But most of the trying and testing has relied upon the enthusiasm and appetite of my husband Maurice, and Alexander and Madeleine, our children —.without their help I suspect I should still be eating my way through all the recipes. I owe a debt to my editors, Morag Robinson and Amanda Hamblin, whose cheerful encouragement and attention to detail has made working on the book a pleasure.

Contents

Introduction	9
Equivalence tables	13
Soups	17
Breads and Rolls	31
Hot and Cold Sandwiches, Fillings and Butters	47
Pâtés, Terrines and Potted Meats	63
Pasties, Pies and Pizzas	77
Salads	103
Well-tempered Travelling Dishes	127
Puddings	153
Cakes, Biscuits and Cookies	173
Drinks	191
Getting It All Together	203
Index	219

Introduction

I can hardly remember an occasion when I've not travelled, like Winnie the Pooh, without 'a little something' in my pocket, basket or car boot. Travelling with my own food started years ago as an economy but now my family and myself do it from choice. I much prefer the freedom of being independent of restaurants and licensing hours, choosing just what I want to eat and when. We find it makes travelling much more flexible and enjoyable, with all the pleasures of the picnic either en route or at the end of the journey.

The idea of Dick Whittington setting off to seek his fortune with his food tied in a red-spotted handkerchief swinging from a stick is a romantic one. Today's equivalent is often a plastic bag of soggy sandwiches. In one's mind Dick Whittington's crusty bread and flavourful cheese or succulent pie is an appetising meal, but so often in practice travelling food disappoints. I hope in this book to help you recapture an enthusiasm for food that has to travel, with a collection of recipes and ideas, tips and advice for a variety of food that can be prepared now and eaten later, whether it is for a packed school lunch, a walking tour or a Glyndebourne picnic.

In these times of spiralling inflation eating out is often an expensive luxury, so much so that the editor of the *Good Food Guide*, Christopher Driver, now reckons that it's cheaper and better to pop across to France to eat! But that is hardly feasible if your destination is Scotland. Travelling today, by land, sea or air, and especially with a family, can still be quite a trial. So the journey itself is likely to be far more enjoyable when the best travelling food accompanies you. And the excited anticipation of a picnic should be matched and surpassed by the excellence of the resulting repast.

Imagination and invention can make travelling food a gas-

9

tronomic experience rather than a way of staving off hunger. But this is not a book about expensive eating — it's about wholesome healthy food that tastes good and gives pleasure; home-made food to be eaten not necessarily as soon as it's prepared but when it is most needed or convenient — in fact home-made convenience food from your own take-away.

I hope this book will serve as a practical primer for the main skills in cooking that will always stand you in good stead for coping with the occasions when food is to travel: from how to make a real pork pie with traditional hot water crust and all the flavour that has long disappeared from the commercially manufactured variety, to how to assemble meals that are more delicious than those in picnic hampers from expensive grocers. How to rustle up soups, salads, breads and pâtés, puddings and drinks, all prepared well ahead. How to keep sandwiches inviting or feed a crowd in the open in the winter. Acquiring this know-how makes you independent of poorly-run restaurants with tasteless food and pubs where children have to stay in the car.

I also hope that this is a book for the times. As we move into the worst recession this century, none of us escapes the effects of inflation and high unemployment and this forces us into an era of self-help. As we enter the less prosperous Eighties economic conditions demand that more packed lunches, more wrapped sandwiches in briefcases, more travelling food destined for office or beach will be necessary. But to do it well needs imagination and I hope this book will help provide you with that and the enterprise needed to deal with these changed circumstances.

One of our leading food writers, Jane Grigson, has written that cookery should relate to life beyond the kitchen. I'm sure none of us would disagree. I hope to show how the arts of the kitchen can attend the practice of travelling, whether for convenience or

10

pleasure, to ensure that all travelling food becomes a movable feast.

But this is not just a fair-weather book. I've included lots of suggestions for year-round picnic eating. There is a chapter on food that can be kept hot, or be reheated, without loss of flavour —.dishes that I've called 'well-tempered' —.as well as plenty of recipes for cold food to tempt the most jaded appetite.

At the end of the book there is a chapter about organising travelling food —.from suggested menus for different occasions to details of containers and equipment for conveying food. There is room for some new design here, but as I write there are signs that this is happening. Some well-thought-out equipment is beginning to arrive from the U.S.A. where the packed meal has been an institution for generations, and from parts of Europe where the climate has always favoured outdoor eating.

If only red-spotted handkerchiefs were easier to find!

Bon Voyage et Bon Appétit.

Geraldene Holt
Clyst William Barton, Devon
May 1981

Equivalence tables
WEIGHT

Ounces	Grams	Grams	Ounces
$\frac{1}{4}$	8	1000	2 lb 3 oz
$\frac{1}{2}$	15	500	1 lb 1$\frac{1}{2}$ oz
1	30	250	9
1$\frac{1}{2}$	45	125	4$\frac{1}{4}$
2	55	100	3$\frac{1}{2}$
2$\frac{1}{2}$	70	30	1
3	85		
3$\frac{1}{2}$	100		
4	115		
4$\frac{1}{2}$	130		
5	140		
5$\frac{1}{2}$	155		
6	170		
7	200		
8	225		
9	255		
10	290		
11	310		
12	340		
13	370		
14	400		
15	425		
1 lb	450		
1$\frac{1}{4}$ lb	560		
1$\frac{1}{2}$ lb	680		
2 lb	900		
3 lb	1350		

N.B. 1000 g = 1 kilogramme

VOLUME

	2 fl oz	55 ml
	3 fl oz	75 ml
$\frac{1}{4}$ pint (1 gill)	5 fl oz	150 ml
$\frac{1}{2}$ pint	10 fl oz	275 ml
$\frac{3}{4}$ pint	15 fl oz	425 ml
1 pint	20 fl oz	570 ml
$1\frac{3}{4}$ pint	35 fl oz	1 litre (l)

1 millilitre (ml)	1 gram (g)	a few drops
5 ml	5 g	1 pharmaceutical teaspoon
15 ml	15 g	1 pharmaceutical tablespoon
1 centilitre	10 g	1 dessertspoon
$\frac{1}{4}$ litre	250 g	$\frac{1}{2}$ pint less 2 tablespoons
$\frac{1}{2}$ litre	500 g	$\frac{3}{4}$ pint plus $4\frac{1}{2}$ tablespoons
1 litre	1000 g (1 kg)	$1\frac{3}{4}$ pint (35 fl oz)

CAPACITY

1 lb, $\frac{1}{2}$ kg loaf tin has a capacity of $1\frac{1}{2}$ pints, 840 ml
2 lb, 1 kg loaf tin has a capacity of $2\frac{3}{4}$ pints, 1.6 l

LENGTH

Inches	Centimetres
$\frac{1}{8}$	3 mm (millimetres)
$\frac{1}{4}$	0.5 cm (centimetre)
$\frac{1}{2}$	1
$\frac{3}{4}$	2
1	2.5
$1\frac{1}{4}$	3
$1\frac{1}{2}$	4
$1\frac{3}{4}$	4.5
2	5
$2\frac{1}{2}$	6.5
3	7.5
4	10
5	13
6	15
7	18
8	20
9	23
10	25.5
11	28
12	30

TEMPERATURE

Electricity and Solid Fuel	Gas Mark	Degrees Fahrenheit	Degrees Centigrade
Cool	$\frac{1}{4}$	200	100
Cool	$\frac{1}{4}$	225	110
Cool	$\frac{1}{4}-\frac{1}{2}$	250	120
Very slow	1	275	140
Slow	2	300	150
Slow	3	325	160
Moderate	4	350	180
Moderate	5	375	190
Moderately hot	6	400	200
Hot	7	425	220
Very hot	8	450	230
Very hot	9	475	250

These conversion tables have been worked out as practical cooking approximations.

N.B. Throughout the book all spoonfuls are level unless otherwise stated.

Soups

A mug of home-made soup, warming the body and the spirit, can be almost a meal in itself. The more robustly flavoured soups travel well and most of them are very easy to make. I find these soups will freeze and by using boil-in-bags individual portions can be stored in the freezer. Most soups can be reheated from a frozen state before being decanted into a preheated vacuum flask or insulated container.

Some people find making soup tedious because of the oft-repeated instructions for basic stock. Not all soups require stock but if you can manage the time to make some basic stocks you'll never regret it because your final soup will be immeasurably improved.

Stock itself freezes well so it's often easier to have a big stock-making session once a month or so and then freeze the results. If you have the time you can amass quite a repertoire of stocks: brown beef, white veal, chicken, fish, light beef, and so on. But if time is short an excellent everyday stock can be made by simply simmering clean vegetable parings with any left-over bones, e.g. from a leg of lamb or a chicken carcase. I use an ice-cube tray to make frozen stock cubes or fill cream cartons to keep in the freezer —.but let the stock cool first.

The pleasure of eating soup is often enhanced by a suitable accompaniment; for example, Wholewheat Cheese Short-bread (see p. 190) goes well with Creamy Carrot Soup or try a Poppy Seed Roll (see p. 39) with Bortsch.

Household Stock

Make sure the vegetables have been well washed or scrubbed, then simply tip the peelings —.carrot, turnip, swede (not potato as it makes the stock cloudy), onion skins, leek tops, celery leaves, whatever you have available —.into a saucepan. Add any bones that you have, or buy some cheaply from the butcher, plus a dozen peppercorns, a bunch of fresh herbs (or a little dried herbs) and cover with water. Bring to the boil, scoop off any scum and discard. Now cover and leave to simmer on very low heat or in a cool oven for 4–5 hours or overnight in an electric slow-cooker. Then strain, allow to cool and skim off any fat that has solidified on the surface. Store in the fridge for up to 3 days or up to 6 months in the freezer. I add salt when I use it. If you are fairly tied to the kitchen it may be easier simply to keep a stock-pot going non-stop. In this case it is most important to boil the stock for 10 minutes each day to keep it sweet and free of harmful bacteria.

Alphabet Soup   *Serves 4*

A quickly made and nutritious soup with a fresh flavour. Use whatever vegetables are available to give variety throughout the year. French markets sell bundles of vegetables and herbs specially for making soup, and some greengrocers and super-markets are doing this here now.

1 oz (30 g) butter
1 small onion, finely chopped
1 carrot, diced or grated
1 turnip, diced or grated
1 leek top or some celery leaves, chopped

1½ pints (570 ml) household stock
4 tablespoons alphabet spaghetti
salt and pepper

Melt the butter in a good-sized saucepan. Add the onion, carrot, turnip and leek and stir into the butter. Cook gently in the butter for 2–3 minutes. Add the stock and spaghetti, bring to the boil and simmer for about 15 minutes until the vegetables are just cooked but not mushy. Check the seasoning and add salt and pepper to taste. Serve with hot rolls or crusty bread.

Dhal Soup   *Serves 4*

This soup is excellent at any time of year and has all the flavour of the curried lentils of Indian dhal.

4 oz (115 g) orange lentils
1 medium onion, chopped
1–2 tablespoons curry paste, depending upon strength
1 pint (570 ml) chicken stock
1 oz (30 g) butter
1 tablespoon flour
salt and pepper
½ teaspoon lime pickle (optional)

Soak the lentils in cold water for 1 hour. Then strain and turn into a saucepan with the onion, curry paste and stock. Bring to the boil and simmer for ¾ hour. Liquidise the soup or put through the finest sieve of a mouli-légumes. Melt the butter in the saucepan and stir in the flour for 1 minute and then add the puréed lentils. Cook until thick. Add salt and pepper and lime pickle if available.

Tomato Soup

Serves 4–6

This soup is nicest made with fresh tomatoes when there are plenty around in mid-summer. During the rest of the year I use tinned Italian tomatoes.

1 small onion, chopped
3 or 4 carrots, scrubbed and chopped
1 oz (30 g) butter
1 lb (450 g) fresh tomatoes, skinned, or 14 oz (397 g) tin
1 teaspoon sugar
2 bay leaves
salt
¾ pint (425 ml) stock, chicken if you have it
¼ pint (150 ml) milk
2 teaspoons cornflour
black pepper
¼ pint (150 ml) single cream or top of milk
chopped basil or chives

Soften the onion and the carrots in the melted butter for 4–5 minutes; don't allow them to brown. Add the tomatoes, sugar, bay leaves, salt and stock. Simmer gently for 15 minutes. Remove bay leaves and purée the soup in a liquidiser or through a sieve until smooth. Return to the saucepan and add the milk and cornflour mixed together. Cook until thickened, season with freshly ground black pepper. Stir in the cream and sprinkle with chopped fresh basil or chives.

Celery and Green Pepper Soup

Serves 4

The green pepper gives this soup a lovely summer freshness.

1 head of celery
1 small onion
salt
¾ pint (425 ml) stock
1 small green pepper
knob of butter
black pepper

Wash the head of celery, discarding any discoloured pieces and keeping back some leaves for garnishing. Chop the celery and the onion. Cook them together with the salt in the stock on medium heat in a covered saucepan for 15–20 minutes. While the celery is cooking, halve, deseed and chop the green pepper. Pour the celery mixture into a liquidiser or a jug and leave a little stock in the saucepan. Blanch the green pepper in the stock for 2–3 minutes. Purée the celery in the liquidiser or put through a mouli-légumes on finest setting. Return purée to saucepan. Add butter and season with freshly ground black pepper. Bring almost to the boil and sprinkle with the chopped celery leaves.

Cream of Mushroom Soup

Serves 4–6

I've seen children who don't like mushrooms devour huge bowls of this soup and come back asking for more.

6 oz (170 g) mushrooms
1 onion, chopped
1 oz (30 g) butter
½ pint (275 ml) milk
black pepper and salt

1 tablespoon flour
½ pint (275 ml) stock, chicken preferably
¼ pint (150 ml) single cream or top of milk

Wipe the mushrooms with a damp cloth and cut in half if small or slice if large. Soften the onion in the melted butter, add the mushrooms and stir. After the mushrooms have softened a little add the milk and some milled pepper and salt. Simmer very gently for 10–15 minutes. Mix the flour with a little stock and add to the mushrooms with the rest of the stock. Cook for a few minutes until thickened then liquidise briefly or put through a mouli-légumes on a coarse setting so that the soup is still speckled. Return to the saucepan, check the seasoning and bring almost to the boil. Remove from heat and stir in the cream or top of milk.

Minestrone   *Serves 10–12*

What a soup! With plenty of Parmesan cheese, a meal in itself.

4 oz (115 g) dried haricot beans
1 tablespoon olive oil
2 cloves garlic, chopped
2 rashers smoked bacon, cut in strips
2 onions, chopped
4 tomatoes, peeled and chopped
chopped garden herbs, especially basil, thyme and marjoram
small glass of red wine
2½ pints (1½ litres) water
2 carrots
2 small potatoes
1 small turnip
2 small leeks
2 sticks celery

2 handfuls shredded cabbage
2 oz (55 g) small pasta or broken spaghetti
salt and pepper
chopped parsley
Parmesan cheese

Soak the haricot beans overnight. Heat the olive oil in your largest saucepan or cast iron casserole and cook the garlic and chopped bacon for a few minutes. Then add the chopped onions and cook until transparent. Add the tomatoes, herbs and red wine and allow to bubble for a few minutes. Tip in the drained haricot beans and pour in the water. Bring to the boil and simmer gently for 2 hours on the stove or in a slow oven. Meanwhile, wash, peel and chop the vegetables. When the beans are tender add the carrots, potatoes and turnips and simmer for 15 minutes. Add some salt and the leeks, celery, cabbage and pasta and cook for 8–10 minutes. Grind in some black pepper, check the seasoning, sprinkle in the chopped parsley and serve very hot with Parmesan cheese.

Spinach Soup

Serves 4

Even people who claim an aversion to spinach have been known to enjoy this creamy soup.

8 oz (225 g) fresh or frozen spinach
1 medium onion
1 oz (30 g) butter
grated nutmeg
½ pint (275 ml) stock
½ pint (275 ml) creamy milk
black pepper and salt
2–3 tablespoons thick cream (optional)

Wash the fresh spinach (leave the stalks on if they are tender) and leave to drain in a colander. Chop the onion and soften in the melted butter over medium heat. Raise the heat and add the drained spinach. Stir for a few minutes and when the spinach is darker in colour and reduced in bulk, grate nutmeg over the spinach and add the stock. Cover and cook gently for 5 minutes. Liquidise the spinach and liquor or press through a mouli-légumes on finest mesh. Return to the saucepan and add the milk, freshly ground black pepper and salt. Bring almost to the boil, check seasoning (you may need a little more nutmeg), and remove from heat. Stir in the cream, if available, as you serve the soup or just before pouring into an insulated container.

Artichoke Soup   *Serves 4*

The smoky flavour of Jerusalem artichokes makes a delicious soup. Try to buy or grow —.they are very easy —.the newer, less knobbly variety.

12 oz (340 g) Jerusalem artichokes, peeled and sliced
1 small onion, chopped
½ pint (275 ml) water
½ pint (275 ml) milk
1 oz (30 g) butter
1 tablespoon flour
salt and pepper
chopped parsley or garden herbs
3–4 tablespoons cream or top of milk

Cook the artichokes with the onion in the water mixed with half of the milk in a covered saucepan. Depending on now long the artichokes have been out of the ground, this will take between 8 and 20 minutes. Test with a pointed knife; they are cooked

when the flesh is soft and tender. Liquidise or sieve the vegetables and liquid to a smooth purée. In the saucepan, melt the
butter, stir in the flour and cook for 1 minute. Gradually stir in
the rest of the milk and then the purée with some salt and
pepper. Cook until thickened, check the seasoning and sprinkle
with herbs. Serve with a spoonful of cream poured into each
bowl of soup, or add the cream just before pouring into an
insulated container.

Kidney Soup   *Serves 4*

From the repertoire of Victorian soups kidney soup is well worth
reviving.

8 oz (225 g) lamb's kidneys — 4 or 5 kidneys
1 oz (30 g) butter
1 onion, chopped
1 small turnip, chopped
1 carrot, chopped
1 stick of celery, chopped
3 fl oz (75 ml) red wine or 6¾ oz (190 g) tin tomatoes
1½ pints (850 ml) stock
bouquet garni of fresh or dried herbs
blade of mace
6 peppercorns
salt

Skin the kidneys and cut into halves to remove the cores. Melt
the butter and brown the kidneys in it. Add the vegetables and
when they are golden pour in the red wine or tomatoes. Allow to
bubble together for a few minutes, then add the stock, herbs,
mace and peppercorns. Bring to the boil and simmer for 45
minutes. Lift out the bouquet garni, mace and peppercorns.
Liquidise or mouli the soup until smooth. Return to the
saucepan, add salt to taste and reheat.

Bortsch

This recipe for Bortsch uses cooked beetroot and thus shortens the preparation time.

1 oz (30 g) butter
1 onion, finely chopped
1 clove garlic, crushed
2 sticks celery, diced
12 oz (340 g) freshly cooked beetroot, diced
4 large tomatoes, peeled and chopped
2 bay leaves
1 tablespoon mixed garden herbs, especially thyme and parsley, finely
  chopped
1½ pints (850 ml) good chicken or turkey stock
2 teaspoons wine vinegar
1 teaspoon demerara sugar
pepper and salt
4 fl oz (150 ml) natural yoghurt

Melt the butter in a good sized saucepan and sweat the onion and garlic in the butter over medium heat. When yellow and sticky, add the celery and cook, covered, for 4–5 minutes. Add the finely diced beetroot and cook for a further 3 minutes. Then add the tomatoes, bay leaves and herbs together with the stock, vinegar, sugar and seasoning. Bring to the boil and then allow to simmer for 20–30 minutes. Check the seasoning and serve with a tablespoon of yoghurt spooned into the centre of each bowl of soup. This soup improves if it is kept cold overnight and then reheated just before serving or pouring into a flask. If you are travelling, take the yoghurt separately and spoon it in at the last moment.

Creamy Carrot Soup

Serves 6

A buttery soup with a beautiful pale orange colour.

1 lb (450 g) carrots, scrubbed and chopped
1 medium onion, chopped
1 pint (570 ml) water
salt
½ pint (275 ml) milk
1 tablespoon cornflour
1 tablespoon butter
black pepper
wholemeal bread croûtons

Cook the carrots and the onion in the salted water for 8–10 minutes until tender. Sieve or liquidise the vegetables with the milk and the cornflour. Return to the saucepan and bring to the boil. Allow to thicken, then add the butter and freshly ground black pepper. Serve with croûtons made from wholemeal bread.

Gazpacho

Serves 4

This famous chilled Spanish soup travels well, I find — to Glyndebourne or the City.

1½ lb (680 g) fresh tomatoes, peeled and chopped
1 onion, chopped
1 green pepper, deseeded and chopped
½ cucumber, peeled and chopped
2 cloves garlic, crushed
2–3 tablespoons olive oil
1–2 tablespoons white wine vinegar or lemon juice
sea salt and a little cayenne pepper
garlic croûtons (optional) — see recipe

If you wish, keep a little of each of the chopped vegetables aside to serve with the soup. In a liquidiser or through the finest mesh of a mouli-légumes make a purée of the tomatoes, onion, green pepper, cucumber and garlic with half the oil and vinegar. Taste, add some salt and cayenne pepper and a little more oil and vinegar, if desired. Chill before serving or decanting into an insulated container. Serve with the rest of the chopped vegetables and garlic croûtons, if you wish. To make garlic croûtons, fry small cubes of stale bread in olive oil and crushed garlic, stirring around to coat evenly.

Chilled Cucumber Soup
Serves 3–4

An excellent cold soup for taking to the races or eating in the garden on a summer evening.

1 good sized cucumber
1 clove garlic, crushed
¼ pint (150 ml) plain yoghurt
1 tablespoon finely chopped mint
salt and pepper (use green peppercorns if you can)
3–5 fl oz (75–150 ml) creamy milk

Peel the cucumber very thinly and chop. Use a liquidiser to make the cucumber, garlic and yoghurt into a purée. Stir in the mint and season with some ground sea salt and green peppercorns. Thin to the right consistency with the milk. Chill thoroughly before serving.

Fresh Apricot Soup

Serves 4

One day last summer while working on this book with my editor we had a desk-top lunch in her office and started with this delightful fruit soup. I also serve it to start a summer meal in the garden.

1 lb (450 g) fresh apricots, stoned and halved
¼ pt (150 ml) water
3 oz (85 g) sugar
¼ cucumber, sliced
1 large fresh ripe peach, sliced
juice of 1 orange
⅛ teaspoon cayenne pepper

or 15 oz (425 g) tin halved apricots plus syrup

Poach the apricots in the water with the sugar until tender. Then tip the apricots, cucumber, peach (leave the skin on), and orange juice into a blender or food processor and whizz to a purée but still with flecks of green cucumber skin. Add cayenne pepper to taste but remember the flavour intensifies while the soup chills. Serve ice cold.

Variation: try replacing the peach and orange with half a melon, skinned and deseeded, for a slightly different flavour.

Breads and Rolls

Bread, the Staff of Life, really does make a meal and for centuries has been the main component of travelling food. At last bread is once again receiving the attention it deserves. In the recent past plastic-wrapped white sliced bread has put many people off packed lunches when some freshly-baked Onion Herb Bread with a wedge of Brie or new Granary Rolls filled with sliced rare beef and home-made pickles would win them round.

Making your own bread is one of the most satisfying and worthwhile activities, with the wonderful baking smell to encourage you and finally the pleasure of eating your own warm-from-the-oven loaf. I hope to show how to make loaves and rolls easily and often quite quickly; not all the recipes need yeast. Golden Plaited Bread, Poppy Seed Rolls or Apricot Loaf, made when you have time, will freeze splendidly like all bread. Loaves defrost in 2–3 hours, rolls in 1 hour in a warm room, but even a slice of bread straight from the freezer can be toasted immediately.

Three Grain Bread (wheat, rye and oats)

This bread has a good crumb and a nutty flavour which everyone seems to enjoy. The recipe makes 2 loaves; we eat one and freeze the other.

1 tablespoon dried yeast
$\frac{1}{4}$ pint (150 ml) warm water
$\frac{1}{2}$ pint (275 ml) warm milk
1 tablespoon black treacle or dark brown sugar
$\frac{3}{4}$ pint (425 ml) tepid water
8 oz (225 g) medium oatmeal
1 lb (450 g) wholewheat flour
1 lb (450 g) strong white flour
8 oz (225 g) rye flour
2 tablespoons salt

Sprinkle the dried yeast on the $\frac{1}{4}$ pint (150 ml) warm water, stir and set aside in a a warm place to foam. Combine the warm milk, treacle and tepid water, pour over the oatmeal and stir. In a large mixing bowl mix the wholewheat flour, white flour, rye flour and salt. Make a well in the centre and add the yeast mixture and the oatmeal mixture. Mix to a dough and knead it on a floured board for 10 minutes. Return the dough to the bowl, cover with a plastic bag and leave in a warm place to double in bulk, 1–2 hours depending upon temperature. Re-knead the dough for 1–2 minutes and divide according to your tins, making sure that the dough takes up about half the depth of the greased tin. Allow the loaves to prove until the dough is just above the top of the tins. Bake in the centre of a moderately hot oven, 400°F (200°C), Gas Mark 6, for 45 minutes. The bread is cooked when it sounds hollow when knocked with the knuckles on the base. Cool on a wire rack and rub over the tops of the loaves with a buttered paper.

GHTF-2

White Bread

This recipe gives 2 small loaves or 1 large. White bread is a misnomer; the best-tasting bread is a creamy colour and I find Jordan's flour makes an excellent loaf.

2 teaspoons dried yeast
¼ pint (150 ml) warm water
1½ lb (680 g) strong white flour
1 tablespoon salt
1 tablespoon mild olive oil or soft margarine (optional)
½ pint (275 ml) warm water

Sprinkle the dried yeast over the surface of the ¼ pint (150 ml) warm water in a small bowl, stir and set aside in a warm place for about 10 minutes until the yeast has frothed. Sieve the flour and salt into a warmed mixing bowl. Add the oil or margarine to the other warm water and pour on to the flour with the yeast mixture. Mix to a dough with a wooden spoon or your hand. On a floured surface (preferably wood) knead the dough for 10 minutes. Put in an oiled bowl, cover with a roomy plastic bag or a hot damp cloth and leave in a warm place until the dough has doubled in bulk. Re-knead on a floured surface for 1–2 minutes to remove some of the air. Shape the dough to fit one large 2 lb (1 kg) greased loaf tin, capacity 2¾ pints (1.6 litres) or two 1 lb (½ kg), capacity 1½ pints (840 ml) tins. Allow to prove again under plastic in a warm place for about 20–30 minutes, until the dough is just above the top of the tin. Bake in the centre of a hot oven, 425°F (220°C), Gas Mark 7, for 30–40 minutes. When the bread is fully baked the loaf sounds hollow when tapped on the bottom. Cool on a wire rack.

White Milk Bread

This bread has a softer dough which is splendid for a plaited loaf or a crown loaf baked in a cake tin. A very popular bread with children.

2 teaspoons dried yeast
2½ fl oz (75 ml) warm water
1 lb (450 g) strong white flour
2 teaspoons salt
7½ fl oz (225 ml) warm milk
beaten egg or milk
poppy or caraway seeds

Sprinkle the dried yeast on the surface of the warm water in a small bowl. Stir and set aside in a warm place for 10 minutes to foam. Sieve the flour and salt into a bowl. Add the yeast mixture and the warm milk and mix to a dough. Knead on a floured board for 8–10 minutes until the dough feels elastic. Place in an oiled bowl and cover with a hot damp cloth or a roomy plastic bag and set aside in a warm place (or stand in a bowl of constantly warm water) for about 1 hour, until the dough has doubled in bulk. Re-knead for 1 minute and form into a loaf.

To make a plaited loaf:
Divide the dough into 3 equal pieces. Roll each piece into a sausage about 12 in (30 cm) long. Press the pieces together at one end and then plait the dough, making sure that you don't stretch it too much. Press the dough together at the other end. Place on a greased baking sheet and brush with beaten egg or milk, sprinkle quite generously with poppy or caraway seeds. Set aside in a warm place to prove again for 30–45 minutes, until swollen and puffy.

To make a crown loaf:
Grease a 7–8 in (18–20 cm) straight-sided round cake tin. Divide the dough into 7 equal pieces (one can be a little larger)

and shape them into balls. Arrange the balls of dough around
the edge of the cake tin, placing the largest in the middle. Brush
with egg yolk or milk and sprinkle with poppy or caraway seeds.
Prove in a warm place for 30–45 minutes until puffy.

Bake either loaf in the centre of a hot oven, 425°F (220°C), Gas
Mark 7, for 30–35 minutes until golden and crusty. Cool on a
wire rack.

Speedy White Bread

By adding Vitamin C (ascorbic acid) to the yeast mixture it is
possible to shorten the time taken to make a loaf as the first
dough proving can be omitted. The crumb won't be quite as
fine as with the traditional recipe but it's a useful method when
time is short.

50 mg tablet Vitamin C (available at most chemists)
$\frac{1}{4}$ pint (150 ml) warm water
2 tablespoons dried yeast
3 lb (1350 g) strong white flour
1$\frac{1}{4}$ pints (720 ml) tepid water
4 teaspoons salt
1 tablespoon sunflower oil

Crush the Vitamin C tablet and stir into the warm water in a
basin. Sprinkle the dried yeast on to the water, stir and leave in a
warm place for 10 minutes to foam. Warm the flour and tip into
a large mixing bowl. Then stir in the foamy yeast and the tepid
water mixed with the salt and oil. Mix well together and then
knead on a floured surface for 5–10 minutes until the dough
becomes elastic and smooth. Divide for baking. I usually make 2
small loaves with 1 lb (450 g) of dough in each small loaf tin.
Halve the rest of the dough and make one piece into a plaited
loaf (see Milk Bread recipe, p. 35) and the rest into a cottage loaf

Take a third of the dough and make into a flat ball, shape the rest of the dough into a flat round and place on a greased baking sheet. Make a dip on the top and press the smaller piece of dough on it. Either press down with fingers to make a dip on top or cut a cross with a knife.

Set the loaves aside in a warm place to prove for 30–45 minutes until the dough is just above the top of the tins. Bake in the centre of a hot oven, 425°F (220°C), Gas Mark 7, for 30–40 minutes. When the bread is fully baked it sounds hollow when tapped on the base. Cool on a wire rack.

Quickest Wholemeal Bread

This bread uses the Grant method where the dough is put straight into the tin after mixing and is allowed to prove only once before baking. This method does save time but the result is more crumbly than when allowing a double proving. The method works just as well if some of the wholemeal flour, say a quarter or a third, is replaced by white flour which will give a slightly lighter loaf, often more acceptable to children.

1 teaspoon dried yeast
½ pint (275 ml) warm water — .blood heat
1 lb (450 g) 100% wholewheat flour, warmed if possible
1–2 teaspoons salt
1–2 teaspoons honey or molasses

Sprinkle the dried yeast on to ¼ pint (150 ml) of the warm water and set aside for about 10 minutes in a warm place to foam. Grease a 2 lb (1 kg) loaf tin, capacity 2¾ pints (1.6 litres) and stand in a warm place. Mix the flour and salt together in a warmed bowl. Stir the honey or molasses into the other ¼ pint (150 ml) of warm water and pour on to the flour with the

37

foamed yeast mixture. Mix together with your hand or a wooden spoon until you have a soft dough. The dough can be put straight into the tin or turned on to a floured board and kneaded for 4–5 minutes and then put in the tin — this will improve the slicing quality of the loaf but it does sometimes mean the dough will take a little longer to prove. Doris Grant's splendid method does produce bread in the shortest time without kneading. Cover the dough in the tin with a roomy plastic bag or a hot damp cloth and set in a warm place to prove for 20–30 minutes, until the dough is just below the top of the tin. Remove from the bag and bake in the centre of a moderately hot oven, 400°F (200°C), Gas Mark 6, for 35–40 minutes. Cool on a wire tray.

Granary Rolls

Makes 12–18

I find this the best recipe for a brown roll. I use either all granary flour — produced by Granary Foods Ltd of Burton-on-Trent — which is a mixture of wheat and rye flour, or I replace one-third of the granary flour with strong white bread flour.

2 teaspoons dried yeast
$\frac{1}{4}$ pint (150 ml) warm water
$1\frac{1}{2}$ lb (680 g) granary flour
1 tablespoon salt
1 tablespoon olive oil
$\frac{1}{2}$ pint (275 ml) warm water

Sprinkle the dried yeast on the $\frac{1}{4}$ pint (150 ml) warm water in a small bowl, stir and set aside in a warm place for 10 minutes to foam. Mix the flour and salt in a warmed mixing bowl and stir in the yeast mixture and olive oil mixed with the rest of the warm water. Use a wooden spoon or your hand to mix to a soft dough. Knead the dough on a floured board for 5 minutes. Return to the mixing bowl, washed and oiled if you have time, cover with a roomy plastic bag and leave in a warm place for about an hour to double in bulk. Re-knead the dough for 1 minute. Divide the dough into 12–18 equal pieces, depending upon desired size. Make each piece of dough into a ball by pulling the dough from the outside of the ball to the centre and then turn the ball upside down when placing on the greased baking sheet. Leave room for expansion or place them more closely together in a greased roasting tin so that the rolls bake as a slab which is pulled apart when eaten (this is a good idea if you want to keep the rolls hot for travelling). Set the rolls in a warm place for 20–30 minutes to become puffy. Brush with milk, if you wish, and bake in a moderately hot oven, 400°F (200°C), Gas Mark 6, for 25–30 minutes. Cool on a wire rack.

Poppy Seed Rolls   *Makes 12*

Use the dough given for White Milk Bread or use your own favourite dough. After the dough has proved for the first time re-knead on a floured board for 1 minute.

To make round rolls:
Divide the dough into 12 equal parts. Shape each piece of dough into a ball by pulling the dough from the sides to the centre on top and place upside down on a greased baking sheet. Space evenly and brush with beaten egg or milk and sprinkle each roll with poppy seed.

To make German breakfast rolls:
Divide the dough into 12 equal parts. Shape each piece into a oval. Place on a greased baking sheet. Use a very sharp knife to make a lengthwise cut down the centre of each roll, not more than ½ in (1 cm) deep. Brush each roll with milk and sprinkle with poppy seed.

39

To make knot rolls:

Divide the dough into 12 equal parts. Shape each piece of dough to a rope about 6 in (15 cm) long. Hold one end of the rope and make a loop to pull the other end through. Tuck both ends neatly into the roll and place on a greased baking sheet. Brush with beaten egg or milk and sprinkle generously with poppy seeds.

Set all the rolls in a warm place to prove for about 30 minutes until swollen and puffy. Bake above the centre of a hot oven, 425°F (220°C), Gas Mark 7, for about 25 minutes. Cool on a wire rack, but of course they are delicious hot from the oven.

Apricot Loaf

One of the joys of making your own bread is that you can indulge in unusual flavours. I find adding dried apricots to a white bread dough gives a delicious loaf, excellent with honey or cheese.

2 teaspoons dried yeast
¼ pint (150 ml) warm water
2 oz (55 g) dried apricots
¼ pint (150 ml) warm water
1 lb (450 g) strong white flour
2 teaspoons salt
1 tablespoon olive oil or softened butter

Sprinkle the dried yeast on to the warm water in a small bowl and set aside in a warm place to foam. Use scissors or a sharp knife to snip the apricots into the other warm water and leave for 10 minutes. Sieve the flour and salt into a bowl. Mix to a dough with the yeast mixture, the apricot mixture and the oil or butter. Knead on a floured board for 5 minutes. Replace in a bowl, cover and allow to double in bulk in a warm place. Re-knead the dough for 1 minute then shape to fit a greased, round tin measuring 6 in (15 cm) across and 2 in (5 cm) deep. Put in a roomy plastic bag and allow to prove for 20–30 minutes. Bake in the centre of a moderately hot oven, 400°F (200°C), Gas Mark 6, for 35–40 minutes. Cool on a wire rack.

Onion Herb Bread

We enjoy *Zwiebelbrot* in Germany — so good with cheese or *Schinken* — and I have worked out this English equivalent. The recipe gives 2 small loaves.

2 teaspoons dried yeast
$\frac{1}{4}$ pint (150 ml) warm water
$1\frac{1}{2}$ oz (45 g) raw onion, finely chopped or grated
12 oz (340 g) 100% wholewheat flour
8 oz (225 g) granary flour
4 oz (115 g) strong white flour
1 tablespoon salt
2 teaspoons dried mixed herbs
$\frac{1}{2}$ pint (275 ml) warm water
1 tablespoon olive oil

Sprinkle the dried yeast on the warm water, stir and set aside to foam. Stir the flours, salt and herbs together and mix in the grated onion. Pour in the yeast mixture and the other warm water with the oil. Use a wooden spoon or your hand to mix to a dough. Knead on a floured board for 5 minutes. Return to the bowl, cover and leave in a warm place to double in bulk. Re-knead for 1 minute. Divide in two and shape to fit 2 greased small 1 lb ($\frac{1}{2}$ kg) loaf tins, capacity $1\frac{1}{2}$ pints (840 ml). Allow to prove until the dough is just above the top of the tins. Bake in the centre of a moderately hot oven, 400°F (200°C), Gas Mark 6, for 35–40 minutes. Cool on a wire rack.

41

Walnut Bread

The walnuts keep this loaf moist. However, it is also delicious toasted or spread with soft cheese.

2 teaspoons dried yeast
¼ pint (150 ml) warm water
1 oz (30 g) broken shelled walnuts
8 oz (225 g) wholemeal flour
8 oz (225 g) strong white flour
2 teaspoons salt
¼ pint (150 ml) warm milk and water
knob of butter

Sprinkle the dried yeast on the warm water in a small bowl. Set aside in a warm place for 10 minutes to foam. Chop the walnuts, but not too finely. Mix the flours, salt and walnuts together. Pour on the yeast mixture and the milk/water mixture. Use a wooden spoon or your hand to mix to a dough. Knead on a floured board for 5 minutes. Allow to prove in a covered bowl in a warm place until doubled in bulk. Re-knead for 1 minute and shape to fit into a greased round 6–7 in (15–20 cm) cake tin. Cover loosely with a plastic bag and leave for 30 minutes to rise. Bake in the centre of a moderately hot oven, 400°F (200°C), Gas Mark 6, for 35–40 minutes. Cool on a wire tray and rub the crust of the hot loaf with a knob of butter.

Treacle Sultana Bread

A soft wholemeal loaf which some people like with a strong cheese and spring onions.

1 tablespoon dried yeast
¼ pint (150 ml) warm water
2 oz (55 g) butter
2 tablespoons black treacle

¼ pint (150 ml) very hot water
1 lb (450 g) wholemeal flour
2 teaspoons salt
4 oz (115 g) sultanas

Sprinkle the dried yeast on the warm water, stir and put in a warm place for about 10 minutes to froth. Melt the butter and treacle in the hot water and then allow to cool to blood heat. Mix together the flour, salt and sultanas in a mixing bowl. Stir in the yeast mixture and the treacle liquid and mix to a soft dough. Knead for 5 minutes on a floured board. Return the dough to an oiled bowl, cover with a roomy plastic bag and leave in a warm place to double in bulk. Re-knead for 1–2 minutes to knock out some of the air. Shape the dough to fit 1 large (capacity 2¾ pints or 1.6 litres) or 2 smaller (capacity 1½ pints or 840 ml) loaf tins which have been well greased. Leave to prove until the dough reaches the top of the tin, about 20–30 minutes. Bake in the centre of a moderately hot oven, 400°F (200°C), Gas Mark 6, for 35–45 minutes. Cool on a wire rack.

Wholemeal Fruit Loaf

Sliced and spread with honey butter (see p. 61), wholemeal fruit loaf is popular with children and is nutritious in a lunch box. I like the loaf toasted —.the smell is gorgeous. For a lighter loaf use all white flour.

1 tablespoon dried yeast
¼ pint (150 ml) warm water
1 oz (30 g) butter
1 tablespoon honey
¼ pint (150 ml) warm milk
1 egg, beaten
8 oz (225 g) wholemeal flour
8 oz (225 g) strong white flour
2 teaspoons salt

2 teaspoons mixed spice
4 oz (115 g) mixed dried fruit
½ teaspoon honey

Prepare the yeast mixture by sprinkling the dried yeast on to the warm water, stirring and setting aside in a warm place for 10 minutes to foam. Melt the butter and the honey in the warm milk. Allow to cool to blood heat then add the beaten egg. Tip the wholemeal flour into a large mixing bowl, sift the white flour, salt and mixed spice on top and stir in the dried fruit. Add the foamy yeast mixture and the milk mixture and mix to a soft dough. Knead on a floured board for 10 minutes. Return to the bowl (washed and oiled, if possible), cover with a roomy plastic bag and allow to double in bulk in a warm place. Re-knead the dough for 1 minute and shape to fit 2 greased 1 lb (½ kg) loaf tins, capacity 1½ pints (840 ml). Allow to prove until the dough just reaches the top of the tins. Bake in the centre of a moderately hot oven, 400°F (200°C), Gas Mark 6, for 35–40 minutes. Cool on a wire rack; brush the tops of the loaves with honey.

Celery and Walnut Loaf

This is a soda bread and is therefore made without yeast. Quick and easy to make, it is good spread with curd or cottage cheese and sprinkled with chopped herbs.

8 oz (225 g) self-raising white flour
2 oz (55 g) wholemeal flour
1 teaspoon salt
3 oz (85 g) soft margarine
2½ oz (70 g) chopped walnuts
2 sticks celery, finely chopped
1 egg
¼ pint (150 ml) milk

Mix the flours and salt together in a bowl and rub or cut the

44

margarine into them. Stir in the nuts and celery. Beat the egg into the milk and pour on to the dry ingredients. Mix to a soft dough with a knife or wooden spoon. Knead lightly in the bowl and shape roughly to fit a greased 1 lb ($\frac{1}{2}$ kg) loaf tin that holds 1$\frac{1}{2}$ pints (840 ml). Bake above the centre of a moderate oven at 375°F (190°C), Gas Mark 5, for 1 hour. Leave in the tin for 5 minutes before turning out to cool on a wire rack.

Welsh Tea-bread

This is my mother's recipe for Bara Brith — a fruited tea-bread containing no fat which keeps fresh splendidly. You do need to soak the fruit overnight in a mug of tea. A good loaf for children to make in the holidays.

$\frac{1}{4}$ pint (150 ml) hot tea
4 oz (115 g) dark soft brown sugar
8 oz (225 g) mixed dried fruit
8 oz (225 g) self-raising flour, white or wholemeal
2 teaspoons golden syrup
1 egg
2 tablespoons milk

Pour the tea into a mixing bowl. Stir in the sugar and the fruit and leave overnight for the fruit to plump up. Next day stir in the flour, syrup and egg beaten with the milk. Pour the mixture into a greased 1 lb ($\frac{1}{2}$ kg) loaf tin, capacity 1$\frac{1}{2}$ pints (840 ml). Bake in the centre of a moderate oven at 350°F (180°C), Gas Mark 4, for 1 hour. Cool in the tin for 5 minutes then turn out to cool on a wire rack. If I am freezing this tea-bread I often slice it first so that the idividual slices can be extracted for a lunch box.

Wholemeal Cheese Scone Round

This is so quick to make that I often bake it just before a picnic and take it hot wrapped in a cloth.

8 oz (225 g) self-raising wholemeal flour
1 teaspoon baking powder
½ teaspoon salt
1½ oz (45 g) soft margarine
1 tablespoon fresh chopped herbs, mainly chives and thyme, or 1 teaspoon chopped dried herbs
3 oz (85 g) grated strong cheese such as matured Cheddar
1 tablespoon finely grated Parmesan cheese (optional)
1 egg beaten with milk to make ¼ pint (150 ml)
a little milk for glazing
1 oz (30 g) grated cheese for topping

Stir the flour, baking powder and salt together and cut or rub the margarine in until it resembles breadcrumbs. Add the herbs and grated cheeses and stir to a dough with the egg and milk. Gently knead until the dough forms a ball and is free from the bowl. Shape into a 7 in (18 cm) circle on a floured baking sheet. Mark into 8 portions with a sharp knife, brush with milk and strew the extra grated cheese over the scone. Bake above the centre of a hot oven, 425°F (220°C), Gas Mark 7, for 15–20 minutes. Cool on a wire rack or wrap in a cloth to keep hot.

ot and Cold Sandwiches, Fillings and Butters

Whichever way you look at it the success of the meal said to have been invented at the behest of the Fourth Earl of Sandwich in the late eighteenth century has been considerable. The sandwich's high degree of acceptability by the British — from the delicate crustless cucumber sandwiches of afternoon tea, to the doorsteps of thick cheese much favoured by teenage sons, and on to the inevitable asparagus tips rolled in thin brown bread of a wedding buffet — has been a *'succès fou'*.

Bread has always been a staple food in the West and the sandwich makes very logical use of it, combining it with some protein like meat or cheese to represent a meal. Whether the move by the commercial bakeries towards the Chorleywood Processed sliced loaf was a precursor or a natural commercial reaction to the popularity of sandwiches with the British I do not know. It is very evident that there is a direct relationship between sandwich eating and inflation — sandwiches can form a cheap nutritious meal. My only complaint is that they can also be very boring. I've decided there are three qualities a good sandwich must have: flavour, texture and colour. How much more 'lovely to look at, delightful to know' is a strong-tasting cheese sandwich made with brown or wholemeal bread rather than white bread. The robustness of the cheese is then matched by the bread, and a layer of very thinly sliced onion or tomato adds flavour and moistness. Although I know of one university lecturer whose wife has made him the same cheese sandwiches every day for eleven years, I think that a large variety of breads and fillings is essential to keep the Great British Sandwich alive.

Fillings for Sandwiches and Rolls

These are some of the most successful fillings which I've made over the years. If you find yourself running a sandwich factory every morning it's worth making up a variety of fillings and keeping them in the fridge. One working mum I know spends one morning a month making a really wide variety of sandwiches which are then wrapped, labelled (often with eater's name as well) and stored in the freezer for the next month's lunch boxes. I have starred the fillings that are also suitable for using in toasted sandwiches.*

EGG AND CHIVE FILLING
These nursery tea sandwiches are always just as popular with the parents. Roughly chop 2 shelled hard-boiled eggs into a small bowl. Add a small knob of softened butter and 2–3 teaspoons creamy milk. Use a fork to mash the mixture until the eggs are finely minced. Season to taste (it's very easy to overdo the salt) with salt and milled pepper and stir in 1 tablespoon of chopped chives.

CURRIED EGG FILLING*
Chop 2 hard-boiled eggs into a small bowl. Mix in 2 tablespoons mayonnaise, $\frac{1}{2}$ teaspoon curry paste and $\frac{1}{2}$ teaspoon garam masala until well combined. I think this is one of the best fillings for toasted sandwiches.

DATE AND NUT FILLING*
Roughly chop 8 oz (225 g) stoned dates and heat slowly in a small saucepan with 4–6 tablespoons warm water. When the dates have softened add the finely grated rind and juice of a small lemon. Continue to mix over gentle heat until of spreading consistency. Stir in 2 oz (55 g) chopped walnuts or cashew nuts. Use in sandwiches or spoon into a pretty dish to serve.

L'AILLADE À LA TOULOUSAINE

Crush 3 oz (85 g) walnuts in a mortar or a liquidiser with 2–3 cloves garlic. Gradually work in 2–3 fl oz (55–75 ml) olive oil until a thick sauce is formed. The fruitier the oil the tastier it will be. This is an hors d'oeuvre sauce from the Toulouse area of France. I like it with celery and fresh crusty bread.

HOME-MADE PEANUT BUTTER WITH RAISINS

Grind 4 oz (115 g) peanuts in a liquidiser or use a rolling pin to crush the nuts in a plastic bag. Mix in 1–2 tablespoons sunflower oil to make a paste, adding it in two or three lots. Scrape the paste into a small bowl and stir in 2–3 oz (55–85 g) seedless raisins and 1 oz (30 g) extra chopped peanuts. For variation add a chopped eating apple or a small sliced banana or a few chopped dried apricots.

PRAWN AND AVOCADO FILLING

Cut a ripe avocado pear in half, remove the stone and scoop the flesh into a bowl. Use a fork to mash to a pulp with 2–4 tablespoons soured cream (or use whipped cream and lemon juice instead). Mix in 2–3 oz (55–85 g) prawns and a little chopped fresh basil (or a little dried basil), season with salt, pepper, and lemon juice or white wine.

TUNA FISH WITH PINEAPPLE FILLING*

With a fork break up the tuna fish from a 7 oz (200 g) tin. Mix in 4 oz (115 g) finely chopped tinned or fresh pineapple and combine with 2 oz (55 g) softened butter or sunflower margarine and $\frac{1}{4}$ teaspoon ground cloves. Season with salt and freshly milled black pepper. Alternatively, combine all the ingredients in a liquidiser, being careful not to make the filling too smooth.

SARDINE AND WATERCRESS FILLING*

Chop a small bunch of watercress and 2 spring onions finely and mix together in a bowl. Add a $4\frac{1}{2}$ oz (125 g) tin of sardines in olive oil, leaving out about half the oil. Mix all together with a good squeeze of lemon juice and salt and pepper to taste.

SALMON AND CUCUMBER FILLING

Wipe, and if you prefer, peel a 4 in (10 cm) piece of cucumber and then dice it. Dry it on paper or in a cloth and combine in a bowl with 7 oz (200 g) tinned salmon, flaked, 2 chopped spring onions and 2–3 tablespoons mayonnaise. Mix together but leave a good texture. Season with salt and pepper. This filling can be extended by adding chopped hard-boiled eggs. It makes a good filling for brown rolls.

MUSHROOM FILLING*

Snip 4 rashers of streaky bacon (preferably smoked) into small pieces and fry with ½ small onion, chopped, in a small knob of butter. After 3 minutes add 4 oz (115 g) chopped button mushrooms, stir and after 1 minute add 2 tablespoons thick cream. Cook until the mushrooms are soft, then add 2 beaten eggs with some salt and freshly milled black pepper. Stir together for 3–4 minutes until the mixture is well combined. This filling is especially good in toasted sandwiches.

LIVER SAUSAGE WITH SWEETCORN AND PIMENTO FILLING*

Liver sausage alone can have a cloying taste; I find this version much more palatable. Melt 1 oz (30 g) butter in a small pan and cook 1–2 chopped spring onions until just tender. Mix in 2 tablespoons tinned or frozen sweetcorn. With a fork mash 4 oz (115 g) liver sausage in a bowl. Add the onion and corn mixture with 1 tinned, chopped red pimento. When well mixed season with salt and pepper and just a little Tabasco sauce unless you like it hot.

SPICED LIVER SAUSAGE FILLING

Add a little curry paste and lemon juice to mashed liver sausage and mix well.

CORNED BEEF AND CELERY FILLING*

Use a fork to mash 4 oz corned beef with a small knob of butter and ½ clove of crushed garlic. Mix in 1 teaspoon strong horseradish sauce and ½ teaspoon Worcester sauce and then add 1 chopped stick celery and 1 tablespoon chopped chives or spring onions. Season with salt and pepper.

SPICED HAM AND TOMATO FILLING*

Finely chop 4 oz (115 g) cooked ham. Skin 2–3 fresh tomatoes by scalding them with boiling water for 1 minute, pricking the skins and then peeling them. Chop the tomatoes and add to the ham. Soften 4 oz (115 g) cream cheese with the grated rind and juice of an orange. Add 1 tablespoon mango chutney, ½ teaspoon garam masala or curry powder, the ham and the tomatoes. Mix to a spreading consistency and season with salt and pepper.

BACON AND CHEESE FILLING*

Grill 6 slices of smoked streaky bacon until crisp. Snip into narrow strips. Chop 1–2 spring onions. Mix the bacon and onions into 4 oz (115 g) curd cheese with 2 tablespoons mayonnaise, 1 teaspoon tomato ketchup, 1 tablespoon chopped fresh thyme (or 1 teaspoon dried) and ½ teaspoon caraway seeds until of spreading consistency. Season to taste with salt and pepper.

CHEDDAR CHEESE AND PEPPER FILLING*

This is a quickly-made sandwich filling which improves a characterless cheese. Grate 4 oz (115 g) Cheddar cheese into a small bowl and incorporate 1½ oz (45 g) butter. Cut a small red or green pepper in half, remove the seeds and cut the flesh into dice. Add to the cheese mixture with whatever fresh herbs are available, finely chopped. Mix to a spreading consistency. This filling is also good with a small onion replacing the pepper.

BANANA, RAISIN AND CREAM CHEESE FILLING

Mash 2 bananas in a bowl with 4 oz (115 g) cream cheese. Add 2 oz (55 g) raisins and plenty of grated nutmeg with a dash of lemon juice or sherry.

Cream Cheese or Curd Cheese Spreads

These fillings are excellent in rolls, sandwiches, in hot jacket potatoes, for stuffing tomatoes, celery sticks or croustades.

Use 4–8 oz (115–225 g) cream or curd cheese as a base, and try adding:

   chopped olives and walnuts
   chopped fresh herbs
   diced red and green peppers
   seeded grapes and chopped cashews
   sultanas and some muesli
   fresh orange and chopped celery
   anchovies and black olives
   whatever fruit, nuts and herbs you have available.

HOME-MADE CURD CHEESE

Make $1\frac{1}{2}$ pints yoghurt from cow's, goat's or ewe's milk (see p. 170). Leave the made yoghurt in a covered container overnight in the fridge. Next day cut the yoghurt curds through with a knife. Drape a really clean (scalded) cheese cloth over and in a good-sized bowl. Carefully spoon and pour the yoghurt into the cloth. Gently gather the corners and edges of the cloth and tie with string. Hang the cloth from a hook, beam or the legs of an upturned chair so that the whey can drip into the bowl. Leave overnight or for up to 24 hours.

You should have 8 oz (225 g) curd cheese at the end of this time. Open the cheese cloth and tip and scrape the cheese into a bowl. This is a lovely smooth curd cheese which can be used for sweet and savoury dishes.

Toasted Sandwiches

Although I can remember my husband and I eating toasted sandwiches in the Cross Keys at Pangbourne over 20 years ago it is only in the last few years that the idea has become widespread. Toasted sandwiches can be a meal or a good pick-me-up while papering the hall. A sandwich can be toasted under a grill or on top of a solid fuel cooker, although it will have to be watched carefully and turned over at the right time. Today the electric Teflon-coated sandwich toasters or contact grills make a quick, efficient job of it. I look forward to the day when every office, school or factory has kitchen/servery units for the use of staff, equipped with batteries of electric kettles, hot plates and sandwich toasters to enable quick meals to be produced. I do know of one enterprising sixth form that has purchased a sandwich toaster for their own use out of profits from running the school tuckshop.

Most sandwiches will toast surprisingly well but because the filling melts under heat it is best to use a fairly stiff filling. I have starred the sandwich fillings which toast well and you will soon find which are most popular and devise fillings of your own.

Sandwiches intended for toasting can be made in bulk, then wrapped, packed, labelled and frozen to save time. Simply allow them to defrost naturally, still in their packing while travelling, and then toast. Or sandwiches can be toasted earlier and eaten cold with a salad when required.

The American Burger Sandwich

To judge from the burger bar in almost every High Street, the American hamburger has made a conquest. Burgers are undoubtedly popular but the standard varies considerably and one can nearly always improve on them at home. The most important requirement is good-quality meat, and if you have a good butcher that is no problem. If you are buying meat in a supermarket always buy the meat with the least fat; sometimes a high-quality finely-minced meat is described as 'ground'. The best and most reliable way of producing high-quality minced meat is to buy the meat in one piece and either mince it at home or ask the butcher to do it for you, in which case it's probably worth making several pounds of minced meat at a go. Most burgers are made from minced beef but veal, lamb or raw ham or pork can be used.

AN AMERICAN HAMBURGER   *Makes 2–4*

This recipe comes from a Bostonian friend and her hamburgers are delicious. She makes 6–8 oz (170–225 g) hamburgers but smaller ones are just as good, especially for children. Raw hamburgers travel well, packed next to an ice pack in a cool box, to be cooked at the picnic.

American hamburgers taste best eaten as soon as cooked, perhaps over a picnic fire or stove or when you arrive at your holiday cottage. But I find some people enjoy hamburgers in rolls, cold in a packed lunch, preferably with some relish.

1 lb (450 g) best-quality finely-ground minced beef
1 teaspoon grated onion
few dashes Worcester sauce
salt, freshly milled black pepper
rolls or rye bread (see recipe)

Mix the beef, onion, Worcester sauce, salt and pepper together in a bowl. Divide into 2 to 4 parts and shape each into a round burger with your hands or use a plain round cookie cutter as a mould, if you wish. Don't compact the meat. If you like, a narrow rasher of bacon can be stretched around the burger and secured with a cocktail stick. Grill or fry the hamburger for about 4–5 minutes each side, depending on thickness and how rare you prefer the meat.

What you choose to eat your burger with is a matter of choice — I like flat wholemeal rolls or soft white baps, but slices of rye bread work well due to the firm texture of the bread, and moderately thick freshly-made toast is also good. Seeded flat hamburger rolls are sold and they are closest to what is usually served in America.

FLAT BREAD ROLLS FOR BURGERS
Both white and wholemeal or granary bread doughs (see pp. 34–9) can be used to make flat rolls that are excellent for sandwiching burgers or other thick fillings. After the proving and the short re-kneading of the dough roll it out on a floured surface to ½in (1 cm) thickness. Use a plain 3 in (7.5 cm) round cutter to cut as many rolls as possible. Re-knead the cuttings and cut more rolls. Sprinkle with sesame seeds and allow to prove on a greased baking sheet for 20–30 minutes. Bake in a moderately hot oven, 400°F (200°C), Gas Mark 6, for 20–25 minutes. Cool on a wire rack.

The Canadian Club Sandwich

As a child during the austerity days of post-war Britain it was a tremendous treat when my mother went off to the kitchen to make us club sandwiches. These two- or four-deck sandwiches still have a mid-Atlantic aura of opulence about them compared with our own single layer ones. Club sandwiches hold together better if made with bread toasted on one or both sides. Allow at least 3 slices of bread for each sandwich. The first slice of toast is buttered and covered with a layer of cheese or grilled bacon topped with a crisp lettuce leaf and some mayonnaise and then the second piece of bread or toast. To complete the club sandwich a layer of ham or a poached egg is covered with sliced tomato and relish or some gherkins and then the final layer of bread or toast. I've never been able to eat more than one club sandwich — it's a complete meal. Wrap tightly in foil for travelling.

Scandinavian Open Sandwiches

Most Scandinavian working lunches are just a half-hour break accompanied by open sandwiches often eaten at the work desk — the French must be horrified — but the sandwiches taste terrific. The wide use of rye bread and fish gives Scandinavian sandwiches a characteristic and refreshing flavour. Tremendous attention is given to the look and variety of the sandwich toppings: some restaurants offer a selection of 200 different kinds. It is important to make the layers of fish, cheese, pâté, or whatever, very thin (it's worth buying a Scandinavian cheese slicer which works well on Edam and Gouda) so that the sandwich can be bitten through easily. I make open sandwiches in England on wholemeal bread, rye bread and pumpernickel slices; these can be topped with cheese, smoked fish, sliced hard-boiled eggs, sliced gherkins, a selection of sandwich fillings (see index), sliced tomatoes, beetroot, onions, cucumber, various pickles and whatever you have to hand that you think suitable. The sandwich ingredients can be transported, by car, packed separately, e.g. for a picnic, and then set out so that each person can assemble his own open sandwiches creatively! These open sandwiches are best put together just before eating.

A French Sandwich

I have seen remarkably few sandwiches being eaten in France — the bread is so good it can be broken apart and eaten straight with cheese or pâté. However, in the south-east of France a sandwich is made called Pan Bagna which is delicious. A long French loaf, or a baguette, or a round *pain de seigle* — if you are all really hungry — is cut in half horizontally. The cut surfaces are rubbed with a clove of garlic and then some olive oil is brushed or poured over them. Thin slices of tomato, stoned black olives and some anchovy fillets, plus some sliced raw mushrooms, artichoke hearts, capers or gherkins, in fact 'les fruits de la région', are layered on to the bread. The

57

other half of the loaf is replaced on top and then a weighted plate is left on the sandwich for at least half an hour so that the filling is pressed in the bread and the bread absorbs the juices. Wrapped in foil and packed at the bottom of a picnic bag it should be excellent for eating by the time you've arrived!

If left overnight under pressure the Pan Bagna can be sliced easily, but whenever you eat it it is really scrumptious.

When on holiday in France we also make what in America is known as a 'Poor Boy', from 'pourboire'. Slice a long French loaf lengthways into 4 layers. Fill the layers with whatever fillings you have, plus some sliced ham or pâté. Cover each filling with slices of tomato, green pepper or cucumber (it always looks more appetising if some is sticking out). Wrap securely in a cloth or foil and keep cool while travelling. Cut into sections just before serving unless you feel hungry enough to eat it all!

Layered Sandwich Loaf

For a special picnic I sometimes make an American layered sandwich loaf. This is a good idea if you have just made a range of sandwich fillings. Take a rectangular tin-baked white or wholemeal loaf. Remove the crusts from the top and the bottom of the loaf, cutting thinly with a serrated knife. Now slice the loaf lengthways into 6 slices. Spread 5 of the slices with a selection of sandwich fillings — vary the colours and flavours to taste good and look interesting. Reassemble the loaf and set in a fridge or freezer for an hour to get very cold. If you wish, more filling or cream cheese can be spread over one or more of the outside surfaces and either chopped fresh herbs or toasted nuts can be pressed into the surface. For travelling it is better to wrap the loaf in foil as soon as it is assembled and then freeze or chill over-night, allowing the loaf to defrost in an insulated carrier on the journey. Serve in slices.

Hot Stuffed Loaf

Either a Vienna loaf or a small bloomer can be used in this way, and individual rolls work well. Cut off one end of the loaf or the tops of the rolls. Remove the soft inside, leaving a $\frac{3}{4}$ in (2 cm) layer of bread under the crust all over. Make the removed bread into breadcrumbs and mix with a strongly flavoured sandwich filling or a garlicky pâté. Check the seasoning and return to the hollowed loaf or rolls. Replace the end of the loaf or the tops of the rolls, fix on with cocktail sticks if necessary. Heat the loaf in a moderate oven for about 30 minutes, the rolls for 15 minutes. For a picnic the loaf can be wrapped in foil before baking and then is kept hot in the foil while travelling.

Alternatively the hollowed-out loaf or rolls can be turned into croustades. The crust can also be removed if desired. Simply melt some butter in a small pan and paint all the surfaces of the bread with a pastry brush dipped in the butter. The croustades are then toasted in a hot oven for 20 minutes before filling them, hot or cold, with a sandwich filling.

Herb or Garlic Loaf

This is a delicious accompaniment to cold meat, pâté or soup. It is highly recommended for English summer picnics where all the rest of the food is cold and the weather has suddenly become the same.

Take a long French loaf, Vienna roll or English bloomer loaf and slice it diagonally across the loaf not all the way through. Spread the slices generously with herb or garlic butter (see p. 60). (Some people, anxious not to develop rheumatism, bury slivers of garlic, too, with the garlic butter.) Wrap in foil and bake in a hot oven for 20–30 minutes, depending on size. Wrap in a warm dry cloth and pack in a hay box or an insulated food carrier. The loaf can be pulled apart for eating.

Seasoned Butters

I find these seasoned butters really useful for spreading on loaves, for baking, to give extra flavour to grilled meat or fish, or for spreading on rye bread or pumpernickel when making open sandwiches. I prefer to use unsalted or slightly salted butter, but it is a matter of personal taste. Remember if you are freezing seasoned butters that flavours such as onion, garlic and salt intensify if frozen for long.

HERB BUTTER
Simply cream 4 oz (115 g) softened butter, 2 tablespoons fresh herbs, finely chopped, and a good squeeze of lemon together until creamy. Season with salt and pepper to taste. *Maitre d'hotel butter* is made with only parsley. *Tarragon butter* is made with only tarragon.

GARLIC BUTTER
Cream 4 oz (115 g) softened butter. Press 2–3 peeled cloves of garlic or crush with the blade of a knife. Mix into the butter with $\frac{1}{2}$ tablespoon chopped parsley (if available) and season with salt and pepper.

MUSTARD BUTTER
Simply cream 4 oz (115 g) softened butter, 1 tablespoon Dijon or seed mustard and salt and pepper until smooth.

ONION BUTTER
Soften 4 oz (115 g) butter and add 1 medium onion, very finely chopped, 2 chopped spring onions (if available) or 1 tablespoon chopped parsley, and salt and pepper to taste.

ANCHOVY BUTTER
Cream 4 oz (115 g) softened butter, gradually add the contents of a $1\frac{3}{4}$ oz (50 g) tin of anchovies, mashed, the juice of half a lemon and 1 tablespoon chopped parsley.

HONEY BUTTER

This butter is quickly made, in the pot you serve it from, if you wish. Soften 3 oz (85 g) butter and then mix in 3 tablespoons slightly warmed honey (I use set honey) until well combined. Because of the honey this butter stays spreadable. It is good on Fruit Loaf (see p. 43).

Pâtés, Terrines and Potted Meats

It has never been easier to preserve meat in these traditional ways. Whether you use a mincer, a food processor or just a sharp knife, some of the cheapest and most neglected meats can be transformed into smooth, rich-tasting pâtés and rougher, firm terrines. And potted meat and cheese, so rarely seen these days, with their concentrated flavours are perfect for eating with bread at any time.

QUATRE ÉPICES

Some readers may wish to make their own quatre épices mixture since it is difficult to find here (I usually bring mine back from France). The proportions of this valuable spice vary a little according to the region but this recipe works well.

7 parts ground black pepper
1 part ground nutmeg
1 part ground cloves
1 part ground cinammon

Sometimes the cinammon is replaced by ground ginger and 1 part of the pepper can be ground allspice (Jamaican pepper).

Store quatre épices in a small screwtop jar and use to flavour pâtés, terrines and other cooked meat dishes.

Quick Chicken Liver Pâté

Serves 4–6

Scrumptious on very thin rye bread followed by a hot onion tart.

2 eggs
1 tablespoon butter or rendered chicken fat
1 small onion, finely chopped
1 clove garlic, crushed or chopped
8 oz (225 g) chicken livers, roughly chopped
½ teaspoon quatre épices
3 tablespoons brandy or dry sherry
salt and pepper
chopped herbs (optional)

To make this pâté really quickly an electric blender or food processor helps. First of all, cover the eggs with cold water and boil for 7–10 minutes. Cool in cold water, making sure the shells are cracked. Peel the eggs and chop them roughly. While the eggs are cooking, melt the butter and cook the chopped onion and garlic for 2 minutes. Add the roughly chopped chicken livers and the quatre épices and cook together for 5 minutes until the juices are no longer pink. Pour in the brandy or sherry and allow to bubble for 1 minute. Remove from heat and put the liver mixture and eggs into the blender and whizz just long enough to give a fairly smooth mixture, or put everything through a mincer on finest setting. Add salt and freshly milled pepper to taste. Spoon into a pottery dish or small pots, cover and chill. Sprinkle with chopped herbs before serving if you wish.

Rillettes

Serves 6

The first stall my children make for in the markets of southern France is the one where golden rillettes of pork are piled high in huge earthenware bowls — in Aix-en-Provence the same stall sells vast loaves of bread, so big it's difficult to link your arms around them, which go so well with the rillettes. Originally from the Loire valley, rillettes of pork, duck, goose or rabbit are popular all over France. I was amazed to discover how easy they are to make. They are quite the best thing to do with belly pork and are truly delicious.

2 lb (900 g) belly of pork
1 clove of garlic (optional)
dried thyme crumbled into a powder
quatre épices
salt and pepper

Trim the rind from the meat and reserve it, leaving as much fat as you can, and cut the meat into 1 in (2.5 cm) pieces, discarding the bones. Put the meat and the halved clove of garlic into a heavy saucepan. Stir over moderate heat, checking that the meat doesn't stick, until the fat just begins to run. Transfer to a tightly-lidded casserole, cover the meat with the rind, and cook in a very slow oven, 275°F (140°C), Gas Mark 1, for 4–5 hours, or overnight in the slow oven of a solid fuel cooker. I use an electric slow-cooker on high for half an hour and then on low for 4–5 hours or overnight. The meat must cook gently in its own fat until the fat is soft enough to be pushed through a sieve, and the heat must be very low so that the meat remains moist and succulent. When the pork is cooked, spoon the meat into a sieve held over a bowl so that the liquid fat drips through. Then use a spoon to press the more solid fat through the sieve. Transfer the meat fibres to another bowl and use two forks to separate them (I find this is the only way to achieve the proper consistency of rillettes). Mix with about half to three-quarters of the fat to give a soft spreading consistency to the rillettes. Season with finely powdered dried thyme, a little quatre épices and some salt and freshly milled black pepper. Spoon into small earthenware pots and either cover with a layer of the melted fat or freeze. Eat at room temperature to savour the full flavour with crusty bread and some red wine.

Terrine of Duck with Orange   *Serves 8–10*

A local farmer's wife rears ducks for the table and sometimes I make this delicious terrine for a special picnic on a birthday.

1 duck weighing about 4 lb (2 kg)
1 lb (450 g) pie veal
8 oz (225 g) green bacon
2 slices wholemeal bread
1 teaspoon coriander seeds
1 teaspoon ground allspice
1 teaspoon salt
$\frac{1}{4}$ teaspoon freshly milled black pepper
2 tablespoons brandy
1 large orange
bay leaves

Use a small sharp knife to cut the flesh from the carcase of the duck. Cut the breast meat into fine strips and mince the rest of the meat with the veal and bacon. Then put the bread through the mincer to clean it and mix everything together. Add the crushed coriander seeds, allspice, salt and pepper and mix in the brandy — this is now the 'farce' or forcemeat. Cut the orange into 6 or 8 thin slices and put 3 or 4 across the bottom of the terrine. Arrange the bay leaves between them. Cover with half the farce, then make a layer of the duck breast meat, and finally the rest of the farce. Arrange the rest of the orange slices on top. Cover with a buttered paper and cook in a bain-marie in a slow oven, 325°F (160°C), Gas Mark 3, for 2 hours. A knife pushed into the terrine will release only clear juices when it is cooked. Remove from the oven and place a weighted plate on top overnight to compress the terrine. Remove the weight and chill in a fridge for 2–3 days before eating.

Terrine of Rabbit

Serves 6–8

I always make sure I've made a terrine or pâté before the holidays start. I also take one with us if we are off to stay at a cottage in the Welsh mountains. We find this terrine of rabbit not too rich for lunches.

1 skinned rabbit
1 onion stuck with cloves
1 blade of mace
8 oz (225 g) belly pork
2 cloves garlic, crushed or finely sliced
12 juniper berries, crushed
1 tablespoon chopped fresh thyme
salt and pepper
8–12 dried prunes soaked in 4 tablespoons Marsala
4–6 oz (115–170 g) smoked streaky bacon rashers
4–6 bay leaves

Place the rabbit with the cloved onion and mace in a pan and add enough water to only just cover the meat. Cook until tender. Remove all the flesh and chop fairly finely. Mince or chop the belly pork. Mix with the rabbit, garlic and juniper berries together with the thyme and some salt and pepper. Add the Marsala from the prunes, stone the prunes and cut each into 3 or 4 pieces if large. Place 3 bay leaves on the base of a terrine or straight-sided pottery dish and line with the bacon rashers. Spoon in half the meat mixture and then make a layer of prunes. Complete by adding the rest of the meat, smoothing the surface level and placing the rest of the bay leaves on top. Cover with a buttered paper or lid and cook in a bain-marie in a slow oven, 325°F (160°C), Gas Mark 3, for 1½–2 hours, depending upon depth of the terrine. Remove from oven and cool with a weighted plate on top overnight. Chill for 1–2 days before serving in slices.

Turkey Liver Terrine

Serves 8–10

Turkey livers are often cheaper than chicken livers and I think they taste better, but this recipe works well with either.

1 lb (450 g) turkey or chicken livers
5 tablespoons port
bunch fresh thyme and marjoram, chopped
4 bay leaves
2 oz (55 g) smoked continental sausage such as cervalat
3 oz (85 g) white or wholemeal breadcrumbs
1 lb (450 g) best pork sausagemeat
4 tablespoons dry white wine
1 clove garlic, sliced finely or crushed
salt and pepper
8 oz (225 g) smoked streaky bacon rashers

Chop the livers roughly and marinate in the port overnight with the chopped herbs and halved bay leaves. Next day put a few livers aside and mince the rest of the drained livers with the smoked sausage and bread into a good-sized bowl. Mix in the sausagemeat, white wine, garlic and salt and freshly milled pepper and the marinade. Line a terrine or deep pottery dish with the bacon rashers. Spoon in half the mixture, add a layer of the chopped livers that you have put aside and then the rest of the mixture. If you still have any rashers of bacon, cover the terrine with those and 2 or 3 bay leaves. Gently cover dish with buttered paper and cook in a bain-marie in a moderate oven, 375°F (190°C), Gas Mark 5, for 1¼–1½ hours. The terrine is cooked when a knife releases a clear liquid from the centre. Remove from the oven and place the dish on a deep plate or roasting tin and put a weighted plate on top so that the juices will run out. Remove when cold and store in a fridge for 2–3 days for the flavour to mellow. Serve with hot toast or brown bread.

Kipper Pâté

Serves 4–6

I sometimes keep quiet about what this pâté is made from until it has been greedily consumed. It's a great pity that kippers have such a poor image — they are delicious and so is this pâté.

4 or 5 small kippers
4 oz (115 g) unsalted butter
juice of a lemon
4 tablespoons double cream
½ teaspoon ground mace
1 pickled dill cucumber or gherkin
slices of lemon to decorate.

Jug the kippers by putting them head down in a jug and covering them with boiling water. Leave for 5 minutes, then remove and scrape the flesh into a bowl or liquidiser, discarding the heads, tails, skin and bones. Add the melted butter and lemon juice. Whizz to a fairly smooth mixture or pound in a bowl. Stir in the cream and the ground mace. Finally add the finely diced cucumber. Spoon into a pot, smooth the surface, prick all over with a fork and decorate with small slices of lemon or serve with wedges of lemon.

Tuna Fish Pâté

Serves 4

Nearly everything for this pâté is contained in a well-stocked store cupboard, so I often make it at very short notice.

7 oz (200 g) tin tuna fish
2 oz (55 g) butter, softened
3–4 tablespoons yoghurt
2 sticks celery, finely chopped
1 small green pepper, finely diced

1 small red pepper, tinned if you wish, finely diced
salt and pepper
lemon juice or wine vinegar

Mash the tuna fish in a bowl with the softened butter. Mix in the
yoghurt, celery and green and red peppers. Add salt and freshly
milled pepper and a little lemon juice or vinegar to give a slightly
sharp taste. If you can, leave the pâté in a cold place — a fridge
or travelling box — for at least 2 hours to mature. Serve on hot
toast or for a packed lunch with pumpernickel or rye bread.

Taramasalata   *Serves 4–6*

This Greek pâté of smoked cod's roe is excellent for a picnic
with fresh crusty bread. If you have a blender taramasalata is
made in a flash, otherwise pound everything together and sieve
for a very smooth consistency.

7–8 oz (220–225 g) smoked cod's roe
3 slices crustless white bread
2–3 tablespoons milk
1–2 cloves garlic, crushed
6 tablespoons olive oil
the juice of 1 lemon
salt and pepper
finely chopped parsley
a few green olives (optional)

Scoop the cod's roe out of its skin and into a blender. Add the
bread, soaked in the milk, with the garlic. Whizz for 1–2 minutes
to purée the mixture. Now gradually add the oil and the juice of
the lemon alternately through the top of the blender. Season to
taste with salt and pepper. Spoon into one dish or individual
pots. Sprinkle with chopped parsley and decorate with some
green olives, if you wish. Chill before serving.

Potted Prawns

Serves 4

If you are taking your own food instead of eating in a restaurant, spoil yourself with potted prawns or shrimps.

8 oz (225 g) cooked and shelled prawns
2 oz (55 g) unsalted butter
¼ teaspoon ground mace
¼ small nutmeg, freshly grated
a good pinch cayenne pepper
a very little sea salt
2 oz (55 g) clarified butter (see recipe)

Check that the prawns are free from shell and whiskers. Quickly run cold water over them in a sieve and dry them on kitchen paper. Melt the butter in a sauté pan and add the mace and nutmeg. Lower the heat and very gently stir in the prawns until they have absorbed the butter. Season with cayenne pepper and a little sea salt. Spoon into 4 ramekins or small pots and pour the melted clarified butter over them. Leave in a cold place to set.

To clarify butter:
Simply melt some fresh butter over a gentle heat. Pour off the clear yellow liquid, leaving the cloudy milk solids behind — add those to cakes or cookies. Clarified butter sets harder and doesn't go rancid as quickly as fresh butter.

Potted Chicken or Turkey

Serves 4

The slightly drier meat of chicken or turkey can stand the added butter used when potting meat. Here chicken is combined with ham or bacon to give a savoury spread for biscuits or toast. This is very popular with young children and I often buy 2 chicken quarters just to make it.

8 oz (225 g) cold cooked chicken or turkey
2 oz (55 g) cold cooked ham or crisp grilled bacon
2 oz (55 g) butter, softened
a little nutmeg
salt and pepper
Tabasco sauce (optional)

Mince the meats on the finest setting. Repeat if the mixture is not really fine. Soften the butter in a small bowl and add the grated nutmeg. Work in the minced meats and season with salt and pepper. If you like a spicy taste add just a dash of Tabasco sauce. Pack into small pots, cover and keep in the fridge for up to a week. To keep longer the pots should be cooked in a bain-marie for 1 hour and then covered with clarified butter.

Miss Parloa's Potted Beef

Serves 6–8

This is my favourite recipe for potted beef. It is taken from a cookery book that my grandmother used when she was a young English wife in Canada at the start of the century. The potted beef is moist and just slightly spiced.

2 lb (900 g) shin of beef
½ pint (275 g) water
2 teaspoons salt
¼ teaspoon ground black pepper
pinch of cayenne pepper
2 blades of mace
6 cloves
bouquet of sweet herbs: bay, thyme, parsley
2 oz (55 g) unsalted butter, softened

Cut the meat into small pieces and put in a casserole with a tight-fitting lid. Add the water and all the seasonings. Cover the casserole and cook in a baking dish of hot water in a slow oven, 325°F (160°C), Gas Mark 3, for 3 hours. Allow to cool in the lidded casserole. Remove the herbs, cloves and mace. Pound the meat and liquid to a paste in a mortar, or use an electric blender, and work in half the butter. Pack into small pots and pour over the rest of the butter, melted, or freeze. Very good with toast or a crusty roll.

Potted Cheese

This is a splendid way of improving a less than mature cheese. It is traditional to add sherry to Cheshire and to pot Wensleydale with port. Potted cheese keeps well in the fridge for several weeks.

POTTED CHESHIRE CHEESE   *Serves 4*
4 oz (115 g) unsalted butter
9 oz (255 g) Cheshire cheese, finely grated
$\frac{1}{4}$ teaspoon ground mace
5 tablespoons sherry
speck of cayenne (optional)

Soften the butter in a bowl and gradually work in the cheese and ground mace. Mix in the sherry to soften the mixture and add a little cayenne pepper if you wish. Turn into one large pot (I often use a wooden bowl) or several small ramekins. Smooth the surface and mark attractively with the blade of a knife.

POTTED WENSLEYDALE CHEESE   *Serves 6*
5 oz (140 g) unsalted butter
12 oz (340 g) Wensleydale cheese, finely grated
$\frac{1}{4}$ nutmeg, finely grated
5 tablespoons port
$1\frac{1}{2}$ oz (45 g) walnuts, in halves or chopped

Soften the butter and work in the cheese, nutmeg and port. Either add the chopped walnuts to the mixture or use the halves to decorate the pot of cheese.

74

Liptauer Cheese

Serves 4

This pink spicy Hungarian potted cheese is very good on rye bread or pumpernickel, especially with a glass of lager. In Hungary you mix the cheese as you eat it, but for travelling it is obviously better mixed first.

5 oz (140 g) unsalted butter
8 oz (225 g) cream or curd cheese
1 teaspoon German mustard
4 teaspoons sweet paprika powder
1–2 tablespoons beer
1 teaspoon grated onion
$\frac{1}{2}$ teaspoon caraway seeds
1 teaspoon chives, chopped finely
1 teaspoon parsley, chopped finely
salt, pepper
2–3 anchovy fillets and a few capers to decorate

Soften the butter in a bowl and gradually work in the cheese, mustard and paprika. If the mixture is too stiff add the beer and then the onion, caraway seeds, chives and parsley. Check the taste and add salt and milled pepper. Pack into one large or several small pots. Decorate with the chopped anchovies and capers. Chill well for the flavour to mature.

Guacamole

Serves 4

An appetising avocado dish from Mexico, with a creamy spiciness which is refreshing on a hot day served with crusty bread.

2 large ripe avocado pears
2–3 spring onions, very finely chopped
1 clove garlic, crushed
2 fresh green or 1 dried red chilli peppers, seeded and finely chopped
   or use 2–3 drops Tabasco sauce

75

1 teaspoon salt
½ teaspoon freshly milled black pepper
1 tablespoon fresh coriander leaves, if available, or 2 teaspoons coriander seed, crushed and sieved, plus 1 tablespoon chopped fresh mint and parsley
1 large tomato, skinned and chopped

Cut the avocados in half. Remove the stones (grow houseplants from them) and scrape the flesh into a bowl and mash with a fork. Add the onion, garlic and chilli peppers and mix well. Then stir in the salt, pepper and coriander and finally the chopped tomato. Spoon into a serving dish. This dish improves if kept overnight in a fridge but the surface will discolour a little. In this case either stir the mixture just before serving or spread a very thin layer of mayonnaise over the top and decorate with pieces of tomato.

Pasties, Pies and Pizzas

This chapter is devoted to pies, from Cornish pasties to Melton Mowbray pork pies and on to pizza, which means pie in Italian. The savoury pie represents one of the peaks of our culinary past and was probably devised as a convenient way of eating meat before forks were in use. What food could be better for taking with you? However, many recipes in this chapter are excellent at any time: Game Pie at Christmas and Pissaladière for a family weekend lunch, for example. I always think of pies as edible parcels that are not only fun to make and exciting to contemplate but richly satisfying to consume!

Cornish Pasties

Traditional Cornish pasties are made from circles of pastry folded over the filling and joined at the side. Sometimes the eater's initials were put at one end to avoid confusion. These substantial pies contained potato, onion, turnip and finally meat. If meat was scarce the pasty became a Tiddy Oggy — a potato pasty (see page 82). Today's pasties contain more meat and less potato and the pastry is shortcrust rather than suetcrust.

Shortcrust pastry:
For 12 oz (340 g) shortcrust pastry:
12 oz (340 g) plain flour
½ teaspoon salt
3 oz (85 g) margarine
3 oz (85 g) white vegetable fat
6 tablespoon very cold water

Filling:
8 oz (225 g) lean, trimmed chuck steak
salt and pepper
1 onion or leek
2 potatoes
1 turnip
egg yolk for glazing

First make the pastry. Sieve the flour and the salt into a generous sized bowl. Rub in the margarine and fat until the mixture resembles breadcrumbs. Use a knife to mix to a dough with the water, and set aside in a cool place to rest for 10–15 minutes before using.

Cut the meat into ½ in (1 cm) cubes and sprinkle with salt and pepper. Slice the onion or leek and potatoes, and dice the turnip. The vegetables keep the meat moist while cooking and help to make the pasty a complete meal. Roll the pastry out to ¼ in (½ cm) thickness. Use a 7–8 in (18–20 cm) plate to cut round to make 4 circles of pastry. Arrange a layer of sliced vegetables on one half of each circle, divide the meat between the pasties, and cover the meat with the rest of the vegetables. Brush egg yolk around the edge of each pasty, fold one half of the pastry over the filling and press down on to the other half at the edges. Use fingertips to crimp the edge. If you wish add pastry initials of the intended eater at one end (this can be very useful if you have someone who can't eat onions, which are omitted in that portion, for example). Glaze the tops of the pasties with the rest of the egg yolk and make 1 or 2 small slits to allow the steam to escape. Bake on a greased baking sheet in the centre of a moderately hot oven at 400°F (200°C), Gas Mark 6, for 15 minutes, then for 45 minutes at 350°F (180°C), Gas Mark 4. Cool on a wire tray.

Minced Beef and Tomato Pasties   Makes 4

I first made these pasties when my children were very young and they delighted in a packed lunch specially prepared for them. They enjoyed the adventure of a picnic alone in the garden, even if tucked away behind the runner beans only just out of sight.

shortcrust pastry or wholemeal pastry made from 12 oz (340 g) flour (see p. 79 and p. 86)
1 tablespoon olive oil
1 small onion, chopped
1 clove garlic, crushed
8 oz (225 g) lean minced beef
6¾ oz (190 g) tin peeled tomatoes, chopped
1 teaspoon oregano
salt and pepper
egg yolk for glazing

Make the pastry and set aside to rest. Heat the oil and gently cook the onion and garlic for 2–3 minutes. Add the minced beef, stir to prevent sticking, then tip in the tomatoes and oregano. Season with salt and pepper and allow to cook gently over moderate heat for 10–15 minutes. Stir well and set aside to cool. Roll out the pastry to $\frac{1}{4}$ in ($\frac{1}{2}$ cm) thickness, cut 4 circles 7 in (18 cm) across by cutting round a plate. Divide the filling between the pasties by spooning the meat into the centre of each circle. Brush the edges with egg yolk and draw the edges together in a join across the top of each pasty. Glaze with the rest of the egg yolk and bake on a greased baking sheet in the centre of a moderately hot oven at 400°F (200°C), Gas Mark 6, for 30–40 minutes, until golden and crisp. Cool on a wire tray.

Spiced Chicken Pasties *Makes 4 large or 8 small*

Chicken makes a good pasty or pie but I like to give it plenty of flavour with spices or herbs.

shortcrust pastry made from 12 oz (340 g) flour (see p. 79)
4 cooked chicken joints or a small fowl
piece of fresh ginger the size of a walnut or $\frac{1}{2}$ teaspoon ground ginger
2 tablespoons mango chutney or lime marmalade
1 clove garlic, crushed
6 cardamom seeds, crushed
1 teaspoon ground coriander
egg yolk for glazing

Make the pastry and set aside in a cool place to rest. Skin the chicken (ideal for the cat) and dice the meat. Peel and finely chop the fresh ginger, mix with the chutney and add the garlic, cardamom seeds and coriander. Spoon over the chicken until well coated. Roll out the pastry into a rectangle and cut into 4 or 8 triangles. Divide the chicken mixture between the triangles and brush the edges with egg yolk. Fold over half of each triangle and join firmly at the edges to make a 3-sided pasty. Make the other pasties in the same way, glazing with the rest of the egg yolk. Bake on a greased baking sheet in the centre of a moderately hot oven at 400°F (200°C), Gas Mark 6, for 25–30 minutes. Cool on a wire rack.

Tiddy Oggy

Makes 4

Traditionally these Cornish pasties contained only potato and were very hard baked — it is said a Tiddy Oggy could be dropped down the shaft of a tin mine and wouldn't break! Today's version is not at all tough but it is still an economical recipe and I have added bacon to balance the nutrition. These pasties are sealed across the top rather than at the side.

shortcrust pastry made from 12 oz (340 g) flour (see p. 79)
2–3 potatoes, diced
1 onion or leek, chopped
8 rashers bacon
1 oz (30 g) butter
salt and pepper
mixed herbs
egg yolk for glazing

Make the pastry and set aside in a cold place to rest. Prepare the vegetables and store on a plate. Cut the rind from the bacon and cut across into strips. Melt the butter and fry the bacon quickly for 2 minutes. Add the vegetables and stir for a minute to coat with the fat. Season with salt and pepper and some herbs, if you wish, and allow to cool. Roll out the pastry to $\frac{1}{4}$ in ($\frac{1}{2}$ cm) thickness. Cut four 7 in (18 cm) circles by cutting round a plate. Divide the filling between the pastry circles, arranging the filling in the centre of each circle. Brush egg yolk around the rim. Draw the edges together over the filling, press together and crimp in a wavy line with your fingertips. Brush with the remaining egg yolk and bake on a greased baking sheet in the centre of a moderately hot oven at 400°F (200°C), Gas Mark 6, for 30–40 minutes. Cool on a wire rack.

Turkey, Thyme and Bacon Pies   *Makes 6*

Now that turkey is available all year round I like to make these pies for picnics — they are also excellent in a lunch box with a salad of French beans. The recipe is for 6 small pies. I leave them in the tins for travelling.

shortcrust pastry made from 12 oz (340 g) flour (see p. 79)
12 oz (340 g) boned breast of turkey
½ pint (275 ml) stock or water
½ onion
4 cloves
1 bay leaf
salt and pepper
1 oz (30 g) butter
6 oz (170 g) smoked streaky bacon, diced
½ onion, chopped
1 tablespoon flour
1 tablespoon chopped fresh thyme or 1 teaspoon dried thyme
4 tablespoons cream or top of milk
egg yolk for glazing

Poach the turkey very gently for 25 minutes in the hot stock or water with the onion, cloves, bay leaf and a little salt and pepper. Cool and then slice the turkey and reserve the stock. Grease 6 pie tins 4 in (10 cm) across, roll out the pastry and line the tins. Cut out the pastry lids and leave them on the floured surface. In a frying pan melt the butter and quickly stiffen the bacon in it. Remove the bacon on to a plate with the turkey slices. Fry the chopped onion in the butter and, when golden and transparent, stir in the flour. Cook together for 1 minute then gradually add the turkey stock and the thyme. Cook until thick, add the cream and taste to see if more salt and pepper are needed. Arrange layers of turkey and bacon in the pie tins and spoon the sauce over the meat. Brush the lids with egg yolk and seal firmly on each pie. Brush with more egg yolk, make 2 small steam vents in each lid and bake on a baking sheet above the centre of a hot oven, 425°F (220°C), Gas Mark 7, for 30–40 minutes.

Beef and Mushroom Pie

Makes 6

Red wine and mushrooms give these beef pies a splendid full-bodied flavour. Served hot after a frosty morning's ride or hike they are most restoring. The recipe makes 6 small pies.

shortcrust pastry made from 12 oz (340 g) flour (see p. 79)
1 medium onion, chopped
2–3 tablespoons olive oil
1 lb (450 g) lean beef, shin or chuck steak, cubed
$\frac{1}{4}$ pint (150 ml) red wine
fresh herbs or bouquet garni
salt and pepper
$\frac{1}{4}$ pint (150 ml) stock
1 tablespoon flour
6 oz (170 g) mushrooms, sliced
egg yolk for glazing

Soften the onion in the oil in a flameproof casserole then add the meat and quickly brown on all sides. Pour in the wine and allow to bubble fast for 1–2 minutes, add the herbs, salt and pepper and the stock. Bring back to the boil, then cover and simmer very gently for 1–1$\frac{1}{2}$ hours on the cooker or in the oven.

Make the pastry and rest it in the fridge. When the meat is tender, blend the flour with a little cold water and stir into the meat juices, allowing it to thicken over moderate heat. Stir in the mushrooms, remove from heat and cool a little. Roll out the pastry to $\frac{1}{8}$ in (3 mm) thickness and line six 4 in (10 cm) diameter pie tins. Cut lids and 6 small fluted pastry circles. Divide the beef between the pies, brush the lids with egg yolk and press on firmly. Place the fluted pastry circles in the centre of each lid, glaze with egg yolk and make a steam vent by pushing a

84

wooden skewer through the centre of each lid. Bake the pies on a baking sheet towards the top of a hot oven at 425°F (220°C), Gas Mark 7, for 30–40 minutes until golden and crisp. Remove from tins when cool enough to handle, or leave in the tins for travelling.

Chicken and Pimento Pie   *Serves 4*

This is a succulent chicken pie which freezes remarkably well. The recipe makes one $7\frac{1}{2}$ in (19 cm) pie and feeds 4. Simply double all the ingredients to make a 9 in (23 cm) pie for 6–8 people. This filling also works well in small pies.

shortcrust pastry made from 6 oz (170 g) flour (see p. 79)
2 chicken quarters or $\frac{1}{2}$ small fowl
$\frac{1}{2}$ pint (275 ml) stock or water
1 small onion
4 cloves
1 bay leaf
salt, pepper
1 tablespoon olive oil or butter
1 clove garlic, finely sliced
2 sticks celery, chopped
1 small green pepper, seeded and diced
1 small red pepper, diced (tinned will do)
1 tablespoon flour
$6\frac{3}{4}$ oz (190 g) tin tomatoes, chopped
egg yolk for glazing

Poach the chicken in the simmering stock with the onion, cloves, bay leaf and a little salt and pepper for 20 minutes. Cool in the liquid, then remove the skin and bones and dice the chicken. Reserve the stock. Make the pastry and after resting it for 15 minutes roll out just over half the pastry to line a $7\frac{1}{2}$ in (19 cm) greased pie plate. Heat the oil or butter and gently fry the garlic, celery and green pepper. When softened add the red pepper. Stir in the flour and cook together for 1 minute, then add the tomatoes and a little of the chicken stock. Cook the sauce for 4 minutes, add diced chicken, check the seasoning and spoon into pie dish. Cover with a pastry lid made from the remaining pastry, seal the edges well and crimp with fingertips or the prongs of a fork. Brush with egg yolk and bake in the centre of a moderately hot oven, 400°F (200°C), Gas Mark 6, for 45 minutes until golden and shiny. Leave to cool in the pie dish and then divide and pack if required for separate lunch boxes.

Sausage and Egg Pie
Serves 6–8

A good economical pie for 6–8 people, excellent for a picnic with a tomato salad. I always add herbs or finely chopped vegetables to bought sausagemeat before using.

wholemeal shortcrust pastry made from 6 oz (170 g) wholemeal flour
    and 6 oz (170 g) white self-raising flour, following the method for
    shortcrust pastry (p. 79) but using the wholemeal flour unsieved
2 oz (55 g) dried sage and onion stuffing mix
3 fl oz (75 ml) hot water
1 lb (450 g) best sausagemeat
1 small leek, shredded
1 stick celery, chopped
salt and pepper
4 eggs
egg yolk for glazing

Make the pastry and rest for 15 minutes before using. Mix the dried stuffing mix with the hot water and leave to cool, or make a little of your own stuffing, if you have time. Add the sausagemeat to the stuffing and mix in the finely shredded leek and chopped celery. Season with salt and pepper. Roll out just

86

over half the pastry and line a greased 9 in (23 cm) diameter, 1½ in (4 cm) deep pie dish. Spoon the sausage mixture into the pie dish and make 4 depressions with the back of a spoon so that there is one in each quadrant. Carefully break an egg into each dip. Roll out the rest of the pastry and cover the pie. Seal and crimp the edges and decorate with pastry leaves in the centre of the lid. Bake above the centre of a moderately hot oven, 400°F (200°C), Gas Mark 6, for 1 hour. Cool in the dish and cut when cold.

Smoked Fish Plait *Serves 4–6*

This fish pie keeps hot happily for a picnic, especially in a hay box. I prefer it just warm. It also freezes quite tolerably.

shortcrust pastry made from 12 oz (340 g) flour (see p. 79)
12 oz (340 g) smoked whiting, haddock or cod
4 oz (115 g) peeled prawns
1 tablespoon chopped fresh herbs, mainly parsley
salt and pepper
1 oz (30 g) butter
1 small onion, chopped
1 tablespoon flour
¼ pint (150 ml) creamy milk
½ teaspoon ground mace
12 green olives, stoned and chopped
2 hard-boiled eggs, chopped
egg yolk for glazing

Pour boiling water over the fish, cover and leave for 7 minutes. Then drain fish and flake into a bowl. Add the prawns and herbs, just a little salt and some pepper. Melt the butter and soften the onion in it. Stir in the flour, cook together for 2 minutes then add the milk and mace. Stir over moderate heat to thicken. Add the olives and remove from heat and allow to cool, covered with a lid to prevent a skin forming. When cool pour on to the fish, add the eggs and taste to check the seasoning. Roll out the pastry to a rectangle about 12×9 in (30×23 cm). Arrange the fish filling along the central strip of the pastry, leaving a margin all around. Brush the margin with the egg yolk and use a knife or scissors to make diagonal cuts 1 in (2.5 cm) apart on each side of the filling. Fold both ends of the pastry over the filling and then lay the strips across each other alternately to make a plait. Brush with egg yolk and bake on a greased baking sheet in a moderately hot oven, 400°F (200°C), Gas Mark 6, for 30–35 minutes until golden and crisp.

Quiche Lorraine   *Serves 4–6*

This well-known quiche is still one of the best, if freshly made. Elizabeth David's recipe in *French Country Cooking* is excellent, especially for eating hot or warm. I find this cream cheese version ideal for eating cold.

Rich shortcrust pastry:
8 oz (225 g) plain flour
¼ teaspoon salt
4 oz (115 g) butter or margarine
2 oz (55 g) white vegetable fat
1 egg yolk
3 tablespoons water

Filling:
4 oz (115 g) bacon, diced
1 small onion, chopped
knob of butter
mixed fresh garden herbs, chopped
2 eggs
2 egg yolks

$\frac{1}{4}$ pint (150 ml) creamy milk
4 oz (115 g) cream cheese
salt and pepper

Sieve the flour and the salt into a bowl. Cut the fats into the flour with a knife, then rub in with the fingertips until the mixture resembles breadcrumbs. Mix the egg yolk with the water and add to the flour. Use a knife to mix to a dough, adding just a little more water if necessary. Make a ball of the dough, wrap in a plastic bag and rest in the fridge for 30 minutes before using.

While the pastry is chilling, gently fry the bacon and onion in the butter for 4–5 minutes, stir in the herbs and remove from heat to cool. Then roll out the pastry and line a greased 8 in (20 cm) flan ring or fluted quiche dish with the pastry. Spread the bacon and onion over the base of the flan. Beat the eggs and egg yolks with the milk and cream cheese, season with salt and pepper, and pour over the bacon. Bake on a baking sheet above the centre of a moderately hot oven, 400°F (200°C), Gas Mark 6, for about 30 minutes. For a really crisp base to the quiche, move the dish to the floor of the oven for an extra 5 minutes or use a metal quiche tin.

SMOKED SALMON QUICHE
Replace the bacon in the above recipe with the same weight of smoked salmon (use pieces which are much cheaper).

ASPARAGUS TART
Replace the bacon in the above recipe with a bundle of just cooked, drained asparagus cut into pieces.

Tuscan Spinach Tart

Serves 4–6

Despite jokes about spinach quiche in cartoons I still make this flan. I like the way this tart is a completely balanced meal.

rich shortcrust pastry made from 8 oz (225 g) flour (see p. 88)
2 oz (55 g) sultanas
3–4 tablespoons red wine (or use milk)
12 oz (340 g) fresh spinach
3 eggs
12 oz (340 g) ricotta or curd cheese
2 tablespoons Parmesan cheese, finely grated
salt, pepper and nutmeg

Make the pastry and set aside in a cool place to rest. Soak the sultanas in the red wine. Wash the spinach well and leave to drain in a colander. Cook for 10 minutes in just the water clinging to the leaves. Stir from time to time; almost all the water will have evaporated by the time the spinach is cooked. Press into a sieve to drain then turn on to a plate and chop very small. Roll out the pastry and line a greased 8 in (20 cm) fluted pie dish or flan ring with pastry. In a bowl beat the eggs with the ricotta or curd cheese. Add the sultanas and wine, the spinach and Parmesan cheese. Season with salt, pepper and grated nutmeg. Spoon into the pastry case and bake on a baking sheet towards the top of a moderately hot oven, 400°F (200°C), Gas Mark 6, for 35–45 minutes until the filling is firm and the pastry is crisp.

German Onion Tart (Zwiebeltorte)

Serves 6

I first tasted this delicious German speciality in the Nahe valley served very hot with plenty of Federweiser, the cloudy yeasty wine from the first pressing of grapes. Even in England, served cold, it is still a great tart.

rich shortcrust pastry made from 8 oz (225 g) flour (see p. 88)
1½ lb (680 g) onions
2 oz (55 g) butter
1 tablespoon mild olive oil
2 eggs
2 egg yolks
¼ pint (150 ml) single cream
nutmeg
salt and pepper

Make the pastry and set aside in the fridge to cool. Peel and slice the onions very finely. Melt the butter with the oil in a heavy based saucepan. Add the onions and cook, covered, over gentle heat for 30 minutes until they are soft and golden. Remove from heat and allow to cool. Grease an 8 in (20 cm) flan dish or tin and line with the pastry. Make sure there is no air trapped under the pastry. Crimp the edges with the fingertips or a fork. Beat the eggs, egg yolks and cream together with a fork. Season with plenty of nutmeg and salt and pepper. Pour on to the onions and spoon into the pastry case. Bake on a baking sheet above the centre of a moderately hot oven, 400°F (200°C), Gas Mark 6, for 30–35 minutes. Eat straight away as a first course or allow to cool.

English Cheese Tartlets

Makes 6–8

Old-fashioned cheese tarts are very good for a snack lunch. Try using some other good English cheeses such as Sage Derby or Red Leicester to give more variety.

rich shortcrust pastry made from 8 oz (225 g) flour (see p. 88)
1 oz (30 g) butter
2 tablespoons flour
¼ pint (150 ml) creamy milk

grated nutmeg
salt and pepper
3 oz (55 g) grated Cheddar cheese
1 eating apple, peeled and diced
2 eggs, beaten
milk to glaze

Roll out the pastry and line 6–8 small pie tins or Yorkshire pudding tins with pastry. Crimp the edges or use a pasta wheel to cut round the rims. Melt the butter in a small saucepan, stir in the flour and cook together for 1–2 minutes without allowing it to change colour. Add the warmed milk by degrees and cook, stirring, until the sauce thickens. Grate a little nutmeg, mill some pepper and just a pinch or two of salt into the sauce. Remove from heat and stir in the cheese, apple and beaten eggs. Spoon into the pastry cases. Use a pasta wheel to cut strips of pastry to make a cross on top of each tartlet. Brush the pastry with milk. Bake above the centre of a moderately hot oven, 400°F (200°C), Gas Mark 6, for 15–20 minutes. When cool enough to handle, remove the tartlets from the tins or leave in the tins to travel.

Traditional Pork Pie   *Serves 6*

One of the best dishes from our culinary past, but sadly the tradition of savoury pie making is disappearing fast. Although the ingredients are very simple, at one time every farm and inn had its own recipe which was jealously guarded. These pies are well worth making especially at Christmas because, if chilled, the pie will keep for 10 days and the flavour and texture far surpass those of any bought pie. This recipe makes one 6 in (15 cm) pie which feeds 6 people. Prepare the filling first and make the pastry when you are ready to use it.

Filling:
1 pig's trotter, split in half
½ onion, chopped
1 carrot, chopped
1 stick celery, chopped
1 bay leaf
1½ lb (680 g) lean pork shoulder
8 oz (225 g) belly pork, skinned
1 teaspoon salt
½ teaspoon pepper
4 leaves sage, finely chopped
knob of butter
egg yolk for glazing

Hot water crust pastry:
1 lb (450 g) plain flour
2 teaspoons salt
4 oz (115 g) clarified dripping or lard
8 fl oz (225 ml) milk and water (half of each)

Sieve the flour and salt into a bowl. In a saucepan heat the fat with the liquid until just melted. Pour at once on to the flour and mix well with a wooden spoon. Then knead the dough in the bowl until the pastry is smooth and soft. Use straight away.

Simmer the trotter with the vegetables and the bay leaf in water to cover for 1–2 hours to make a good stock. Strain and return to the saucepan and boil steadily until ½ pint (275 ml) remains. Cool and allow to set. Cut the lean pork and belly pork into ½ in (1 cm) dice. Mix in the salt, pepper and finely chopped sage. Make the hot water crust pastry (see above) and roll out two-thirds to line a greased 6 in (15 cm) loose-bottomed cake tin, leaving the dough protruding over the rim. Pack the meat into the pastry case firmly and dot with the butter. Cut the pastry level with the rim of the cake tin. Roll out the rest of the pastry, stand the cake tin on it and cut around it to make the lid of the pie. Brush the pastry edge with water and place over the meat, pressing the pastry edges together to seal well. Crimp with the back of a knife and make a good hole in the centre of the lid to allow steam to escape. Roll out the pastry trimmings and cut some leaves to decorate the pie and brush with the egg yolk. Bake in the centre of a moderately hot oven, 400°F (200°C), Gas Mark 6, for 30 minutes. Reduce the heat to 350°F (180°C), Gas Mark 4, and bake for a further 1½ hours. Allow to cool in the tin for 15 minutes. Heat the jellied stock to almost boiling, season with salt and pepper and pour through the hole in the lid of the pie, using a small funnel or an icing nozzle. Allow to cool completely, then remove from tin or leave in the tin for travelling.

Veal and Ham Pie

Serves 8

I make a veal and ham pie after Christmas when what's left of a gammon will go into this pie along with some pie veal (I always keep some in the freezer). This recipe makes a 7 in (18 cm) pie but, if you wish, a larger pie can be made by adding 2 or 3 hard-boiled eggs and baking the pie in a long loaf tin.

1 pig's trotter, split in half
½ onion, chopped
1 carrot, chopped
1 stick celery, chopped
1 bay leaf
1¼ lb (560 g) ham, including some fat
1 lb (450 g) pie veal
salt and pepper (be sparing)
1 tablespoon chopped fresh thyme
knob of butter
hot water crust pastry made from 1¼ lb (560 g) flour, 2 teaspoons salt, 5 oz (140 g) clarified dripping or lard and ½ pint (275 ml) milk and water (see method on p. 93)
egg yolk for glazing

Make the jellied stock from the trotter, vegetables and herbs as in the previous recipe. Dice the ham and pie veal, season

94

cautiously and mix in the chopped thyme. Make the pastry and line a 7 in (18 cm) round loose-bottomed cake tin. Pack in the meat and dot with the butter. Cover with the pastry as in the pork pie recipe. Brush with the egg yolk and bake in a moderately hot oven at 400°F (200°C), Gas Mark 6, for 30 minutes and then for 2 hours at 350°F (180°C), Gas Mark 4. Cool for 15 minutes and then pour in the hot seasoned stock through the steam vent in the lid of the pie, using a small funnel or icing nozzle. Allow to cool completely before serving.

Game Pie

Serves 8–10

My game pie is usually dependent upon neighbouring farmers being good shots. A mixture of pigeon, pheasant, venison, or whatever you can rustle up, eked out with some chicken, turkey or guinea fowl with perhaps some kidney will make an excellent pie. I usually include some mushrooms and streaky bacon. This recipe makes a 10 × 4 in (25 × 10 cm) pie that slices well.

1 pig's trotter, split in half
½ onion, chopped
1 carrot, chopped
1 stick celery, chopped
1 bay leaf
bouquet garni
2 lb (900 g) mixed game meat, diced
4 smoked streaky bacon rashers, diced
1 or 2 lamb's kidneys, cored and diced
4 oz (115 g) mushrooms, sliced
2 tablespoons chopped parsley
½ teaspoon mace
salt and pepper
2 wine glasses port or red wine
hot water crust pastry as for Veal and Ham Pie (see p. 94)
egg yolk for glazing

Make a jellied stock with the trotter, vegetables and herbs (see p.

93). Strain and reduce to ½ pint (275 ml) and season well with pepper and salt. Cut all the meats into ¼–½ in (½–1 cm) pieces. Mix with the bacon, kidney, mushrooms, parsley, mace and salt and pepper. Make the hot water crust pastry and line a greased 10 × 4 in (25 × 10 cm) loaf tin with pastry or use an oval raised pie mould, if you have one. Pack in the meat, pour over the port or wine and cover with a pastry lid. Make 3 or 4 steam vents and decorate with pastry leaves and berries made from pastry trimmings. Brush with egg yolk and bake in a moderately hot oven, 400°F (200°C), Gas Mark 6, for 30 minutes and for 2 hours at 350°F (180°C), Gas Mark 4. Cool for 15 minutes and then pour the hot stock through the steam vents using a small funnel or icing nozzle. Serve cold.

Basic Pizza Dough

This is my favourite pizza dough but I find most plain white bread doughs work quite well. I would use a wholemeal bread dough with caution as it needs a very strong flavoured pizza topping to balance the robust taste of the dough. This recipe gives enough dough to make two 9 in (23 cm) pizzas which will each serve 2 people or 1 very hungry mortal. I prefer to use strong bread flour but you may find the dough is easier to handle if made with ordinary plain flour and is more like a true Italian pizza.

8 oz (225 g) strong white flour
1 teaspoon salt
½ oz (15 g) fresh yeast or 1 teaspoon dried yeast
¼ pint (150 ml) warm water
1 tablespoon olive oil

Sieve the flour and salt into a bowl and set aside in a warm place. Cream the fresh yeast with half the water or spinkle the dried yeast on to half the water and leave in a warm place to froth. (I don't add sugar to the yeast but if you feel the yeast needs 'feeding' add a teaspoon of sugar to the yeast solution.) After 5–10 minutes and when the yeast has started to froth, add the rest of the water and tip into the flour with the oil. Use a wooden spoon to mix together well. Then knead the dough into a ball. Turn on to a floured board and knead for 5 minutes until the dough acquires more spring. It will feel firmer and more elastic and the surface will start to feel cooler because of the chemical activity of the yeast. Rinse out the bowl with warm water and dry it. Rub a little olive oil over the inside of the bowl, place the dough in the bowl and cover with a warm damp cloth or a roomy plastic bag. Leave in a warm place or stand the bowl in another holding warm water (check that the water stays warm) for about an hour until the dough has doubled in size. If you wish, the dough can be stored overnight in the fridge and then allowed to double in size in a warm place when you need to use it. Turn the dough on to a very slightly floured surface and knead very gently for 1 minute to knock it down to original size and to distribute the air bubbles evenly. The dough is now ready for use. Roll out to fit the tins as directed in each recipe, spread with sauce and garnish. Leave for 15–20 minutes for the dough to start rising, then bake towards the top of a hot oven at 425°F (220°C), Gas Mark 7, for 25–30 minutes.

Speedy Pizza Dough

This is a scone-like base which does at least enable one to produce a pizza at short notice, especially if you have some pizza tomato sauce already in the fridge.

8 oz (225 g) self-raising flour
1 teaspoon salt
2 oz (55 g) butter or margarine
1 egg mixed with milk to make $\frac{1}{4}$ pint (150 ml)

97

Sieve the flour and salt into a bowl. Cut the butter or margarine into the flour with a knife, then rub in with the fingertips until it resembles breadcrumbs. Mix to a dough with the liquid. Knead into a ball with one hand. Pat into shape on a floured board, and fit into 2 greased 9 in (23 cm) pizza tins or sandwich tins. Now spread with pizza sauce, garnish, and bake above the centre of a hot oven, 425°F (220°C), Gas Mark 7, for 20–25 minutes.

Tomato Pizza Sauce   *Covers two 9 in pizzas*

Italian pizzas are delicious with this aromatic sauce as a base for anchovies, olives, mussels or whatever your garnish. If you have plenty of fresh tomatoes use them peeled, otherwise tinned Italian tomatoes work well.

1 tablespoon olive oil (the fruitier the better)
2 onions, sliced and chopped
2 cloves garlic, crushed
15 oz (425 g) fresh or tinned tomatoes, peeled and chopped
$\frac{1}{2}$ teaspoon sugar
marjoram or oregano, fresh or dried
thyme
1 bay leaf
salt and pepper

Heat the oil in a heavy based saucepan and gently cook the onions and garlic in it for 5–6 minutes. Tip in the tomatoes, sugar, marjoram and thyme (according to taste), bay leaf (cut in two) and some salt and pepper. Bring up to the boil, stir and then lower the heat so that the sauce just simmers for 25–30 minutes. Stir from time to time and when ready the sauce will be thick and aromatic. Cool a little before using. This sauce will keep in a lidded container in the fridge for up to a week.

Pizza Napoletana

Serves 2–4

Probably the most well-known pizza, it's none the less a very good one. The recipe makes two 9 in (23 cm) pizzas.

basic Pizza Dough made with 8 oz (225 g) flour (see p. 96)
Tomato Pizza Sauce (see p. 98)
1¾ oz (50 g) tin anchovy fillets
14 black olives
2–4 oz (55–115 g) Mozzarella or grated Cheddar cheese
sprinkling of Parmesan cheese

Grease two 9 in (23 cm) pizza or tart tins. Divide the dough in two and flatten it into the tins (if that is a problem, gently roll out the dough to fit and press into the tins). Spread each pizza with tomato sauce almost to the edges. Decorate with the anchovy fillets. I run them under warm water and then cut the wider ones into narrow strips. I usually arrange them like the spokes of a wheel to give 6 sections of pizza. Place an olive in each section and one in the middle. Sprinkle with the cheeses, leave to rise, and bake as directed on p. 97. Eat straight away followed by a crisp, garlicky salad or cool and pack.

Bacon and Celery Pizza

Serves 2–4

This is useful for people who don't like anchovies or cheese. Use the recipe above, replacing the anchovies with strips of streaky bacon, and the cheese with chopped celery.

Mushroom Pizza

Makes 10–12 portions

For packed lunches and parties I often make large rectangular pizzas and then cut them into oblong portions like those in a Provençal boulangerie.

basic Pizza Dough made with 8 oz (225 g) flour (see p. 96)
Tomato Pizza Sauce (see p. 98)
6–8 oz (170–225 g) mushrooms, button if possible
1 tablespoon olive oil
1 tablespoon butter
2 oz (55 g) smoked continental sausage, diced

Grease a swiss roll tin 13 × 9 in (32 × 23 cm). Roll out the dough to fit and press into the tin. Wipe and then slice the mushrooms and cook gently in a frying pan in the oil and butter. Remove from the heat and cover so that the mushrooms stay juicy. Spread the tomato sauce on the dough. Arrange the mushrooms evenly over the surface and sprinkle with the diced sausage. Prove and bake as directed on p. 97. Cut into 10 or 12 wedges for serving.

Ham and Red Pepper Pizza

Makes 12 portions

Another good pizza for crowds.

In the above recipe replace mushrooms with strips of red pepper (use fresh, tinned or bottled) arranged in a lattice pattern over the dough, and sprinkle with 4 oz (115 g) chopped cooked ham. Stud each diamond of the lattice with an olive.

Pissaladière

For a pizza without tomatoes I enjoy the Provençal pizza, rich with onions and black olives — all one needs to contemplate while munching is a little village square, high in the Var, busy with market stalls.

basic Pizza Dough made with 8 oz (225 g) flour (see p. 96)
1½ lb (680 g) onions
2 cloves garlic
3 tablespoons olive oil
1¾ oz (50 g) tin anchovy fillets
12–14 black olives
salt and pepper

Peel and very thinly slice the onions; chop the garlic finely. Heat the olive oil in a heavy based saucepan. Cook the onions and garlic, covered, over low heat for 30 minutes until they are soft and mushy but still golden. Set aside to cool. Drain the anchovies (rinse quickly in warm water if you find them too salty) and separate the fillets on a saucer. Grease a swiss roll tin 13 × 9 in (32 × 23 cm) and roll out the dough to fit. Press into the tin and spread the onions over the dough. Make a lattice pattern with the anchovies, cutting the wide ones if necessary, and dot the grid with the black olives. Prove and bake as directed on p. 97. Cut into wedges for serving.

Tuna with Capers Pizza

I make this large pizza in a round, loose-bottomed French tart tin — they are now quite widely available in this country. For picnics or outdoor parties the pizza can be served on the tin base.

basic Pizza Dough made with 8 oz (225 g) flour (see p. 96)
Tomato Pizza Sauce (see p. 98)
7 oz (200 g) tin tuna fish
salt and freshly milled pepper
mixed fresh herbs, finely chopped
1 Spanish onion
1 tablespoon olive oil
1 tablespoon capers

Grease a 12 in (30 cm) diameter tin and roll out the pizza dough
to fit, then press gently into the tin. Spread with the tomato
sauce. Drain the oil from the tinned tuna fish and give to the cat.
Flake the fish roughly into a bowl and sprinkle with salt, pepper
and the herbs. Slice the peeled onion into a soup bowl, separate
the slices into rings and pour over the olive oil. Distribute the fish
over the pizza and sprinkle with the capers. Arrange the onion
rings over the pizza. Leave in a warm place for 20–30 minutes to
allow the dough to get puffy. Bake towards the top of a hot
oven, 425°F (220°C), Gas Mark 7, for 25–30 minutes.

Salads

For me a salad can be a meal in itself — a cool tomato salad, glistening with olive oil and strewn with chopped fresh basil, only needs some crusty French bread and a little Brie to make a perfect picnic lunch. A salad must always be tempting, and should taste as good as it looks. Salads for travelling need careful thought. I wouldn't recommend a lettuce-based salad unless you can keep the lettuce crisp and cold in an icebox. Obviously those salads that have the dressing added at an early stage are good, as are those like a dried bean salad which improve with steeping. If you can, chill the salad well before packing it, covered, in an insulated food box next to an ice pack. If tossing the salad just before serving, pack the dressing separately in a wide-necked screw-topped jar or a small lidded plastic container.

I make a very wide range of salads and dressings and although some salads, e.g. Salade Niçoise, benefit from a great number of ingredients, I think it's often better not to throw absolutely everything you have to hand into the salad. Let each salad retain its own identity — restraint is often more effective than abundance in cooking.

Here are some of the most useful salad dressings. Try adaptations of your own; for example, mix some blue cheese (Roquefort is best but desperately expensive) into the soured cream dressing and try it on a dish of prawns with fresh pineapple. A marvellous combination!

How much dressing you apply to a salad is a matter of personal taste, so you may sometimes prefer to double or even treble, in the case of rice salads, the given recipes for salad dressings.

Sauce Vinaigrette

The classic French salad dressing.

1 tablespoon wine vinegar, red or white
salt (rock salt is best)
black pepper, freshly ground
4–6 tablespoons olive oil
1 tablespoon fresh garden herbs, finely chopped (optional)

Measure the vinegar, using whichever colour is appropriate, into a small jug or bowl and grind in some salt and pepper. Add the oil and stir briskly. Sprinkle in the herbs and stir again. Or put all the ingredients, except the herbs, in a screw-topped jar, shake vigorously and add the herbs just before using. The more oil is added the less sharp the dressing.

French Dressing

A variation of Sauce Vinaigrette, often preferred by Americans.

1 tablespoon wine vinegar
salt and black pepper
1 teaspoon brown sugar or honey
1 teaspoon Dijon mustard
4–6 tablespoons olive oil
1 tablespoon fresh herbs, finely chopped

Measure the vinegar into a small jug and mix in the salt, pepper, sugar and mustard. Stir in the olive oil vigorously and then add the herbs. Stir well before using.

Mayonnaise

One of the most delicious and versatile salad dressings, you can build a salad around it especially if you make Aïoli.

1 large egg yolk
¼ teaspoon dry mustard (optional)
¼ pint (150 ml) olive oil
1 tablespoon white wine vinegar or lemon juice
salt and pepper

I use my best olive oil for mayonnaise, and only add mustard if the oil isn't fruity — some people find the addition of dry mustard helps to prevent the mayonnaise curdling. All the ingredients need to be warm, and I leave the oil in the sun for an hour. In a warm dry bowl beat the egg yolk with the mustard, salt and pepper. Now add 1 drop of oil and beat it in with a wooden spoon or a wire whisk. Continue adding the oil in drops, beating it in each time until you can feel and see the mixture thicken and turn a lighter colour. Now the oil can be added in teaspoonfuls — but start it gradually. Finally the oil may be added in a very thin trickle. When all the oil has been added add the wine vinegar to taste and check the seasoning.

If the mayonnaise curdles, the only way to save it is to start again with another egg yolk. Add the mustard, salt and pepper and add a second ¼ pint (150 ml) oil in an even more gradual fashion. When half the oil has been added gradually, add teaspoonfuls of the curdled mixture alternately with the oil, and finally add the vinegar. You will have double your originally desired quantity but it will keep for a week, covered, in a fridge. Making mayonnaise in a liquidiser is simplicity itself, but start with a *whole* egg. Put the egg, mustard, salt and pepper into the liquidiser, cover and whizz for 3 seconds. Then, with the liquidiser on its lowest setting, pour the oil in a thin stream through the opening in the lid on to the egg. Whizz until the mixture is thick and all the oil has been added. Finally add the vinegar.

Aïoli

The Provençal mayonnaise. If you like garlic you'll find it addictive. Excellent with cold fish.

2 (or more!) cloves garlic
1 large egg yolk
¼ teaspoon dry mustard (optional)
salt and pepper
¼ pint (150 ml) fruity olive oil (a green Provençal oil is best)
just a squeeze of lemon juice

Peel and crush the cloves of garlic using the flat blade of a knife or a garlic crusher. Mix with the egg yolk, mustard, salt and pepper. Then add oil as for Mayonnaise, and finally the lemon juice.

Yoghurt and Lemon Dressing

This is my emergency dressing if the stocks of olive oil are low. It's good for slimmers and is excellent on grated root vegetables.

2 squeezes lemon juice
salt and pepper
4 tablespoons home-made or natural yoghurt
a little grated lemon rind
mixed fresh herbs (especially mint), finely chopped

Mix the lemon juice with the salt and pepper. Stir in the yoghurt and sprinkle the finely grated lemon rind and herbs into the mixture.

Cream Cheese Dressing

Definitely not for slimmers, this American salad dressing has a bitter sweetness which goes well with watercress, landcress, onions and eggs.

1 clove garlic
salt and pepper
¼ teaspoon Dijon mustard
1 tablespoon lemon juice or white wine vinegar
2 tablespoons top of milk
4 tablespoons cream cheese

Peel and crush the garlic with the salt, add the pepper, mustard and lemon juice or vinegar. Mix 1 tablespoon of milk into the cream cheese to soften it. Stir the cream cheese gradually into the seasoned mixture. Thin to the required consistency with a little extra milk.

Soured Cream Dressing

A very popular salad dressing in Germany, excellent with gherkins and smoked sausage or fish.

1 teaspoon finely chopped shallot or mild onion
salt and pepper
¼ teaspoon German mustard
1 tablespoon lemon juice or wine vinegar
4 tablespoons soured cream
mixed fresh herbs, finely chopped

Mix the shallot with the salt, pepper and mustard. Moisten with the lemon juice or vinegar and stir in the soured cream and herbs.

Canadian Cooked Salad Dressing

As children we always preferred this less sharp dressing for hot potatoes or crisp lettuce.

2 tablespoons plain flour
1 tablespoon butter
1 tablespoon granulated sugar
2 teaspoons dry mustard
1 teaspoon salt
1 egg yolk
7 fl oz (200 ml) milk
2 fl oz (50 ml) white wine vinegar, or less according to taste
1 tablespoon cream
black pepper

Measure the flour, butter, sugar, mustard, salt and egg yolk into a double boiler or small heavy-based saucepan. Mix to a paste with a little of the milk. Gradually add the rest of the milk and stir over moderate heat until the mixture starts to thicken. Slowly add the vinegar, stirring all the time until the consistency is like pouring cream. Cook for 4–5 minutes all together. Remove from heat and beat in the cream and pepper. Pour into a jug or bowl to cool.

My mother notes that the salad dressing will keep closely covered in a fridge for a week and during the war she omitted the egg and has done so ever since!

Broad Bean Salad   *Serves 4*

Salads of new young summer vegetables are always a treat; broad beans (even in their pods if they are still very small), baby carrots, French beans and fingerwidth runner beans are all delicious this way. It is important to add the dressing straight away to cooked or blanched vegetables so that they can absorb the flavour of the dressing as effectively as possible.

1 lb (450 g) young broad beans, shelled weight
1 clove garlic
1 shallot, finely chopped
1 tablespoon summer savory, finely chopped
Sauce Vinaigrette (see p. 105)

Plunge the broad beans into boiling salted water for 2 minutes; older beans may need 4–5 minutes. Rub a bowl with the clove of garlic. Drain the beans and tip into the bowl. Stir in the shallot and the finely chopped summer savory (known in Germany as bean herb because it always accompanies broad beans — it will keep blackfly away from beans if grown beside them). Pour over the dressing and, if you can stop yourself gobbling up these lovely beans, leave for 30 minutes before serving.

Tomato Salad   *Serves 4*

This is a summer salad for when the tomatoes taste of the sun and fresh basil is around.

1 lb (450 g) large firm tomatoes (I grow Mamande)
1 clove garlic
1 shallot, finely chopped
handful of fresh basil or equal parts of parsley and mint, finely
   chopped
Sauce Vinaigrette (see p. 105)

Pour boiling water over the tomatoes. Nick their skins with a pointed knife and the skins will start to shrink off. Drain and peel the tomatoes and slice across as thinly as you can. Rub a pottery dish with the halved clove of garlic (I crush it into the bowl). Put layers of tomatoes sprinkled with the shallot and the basil into the bowl. Pour the dressing over and allow to stand for at least 2 hours for the flavours to combine.

Carrot Salad

This is my economy salad. It must be the cheapest of all to make (unless you have masses of vegetables in the garden). The sweetness of the carrots contrasts well with the yoghurt dressing and I find children love this salad.

½–1 lb (¼–½ kg) carrots
handful seedless raisins
Yoghurt Dressing (see p. 107)

Wash and thinly peel the carrots; if using new carrots simply scrub them. Grate the carrots finely into a bowl and mix in the raisins. Stir in the dressing and leave for at least 30 minutes before serving.

A variation is to use half raw carrots and half raw turnip — this gives the salad a beautiful colour and a slightly sharper taste.

Spinach Salad

Serves 4

Young fresh spinach makes an excellent salad but since it is best prepared at the last moment I think, for travelling, a salad of cooked spinach is preferable.

1½ lb (680 g) fresh spinach
grated nutmeg
2 hard-boiled eggs
Cream Cheese Dressing (see p. 108)

Wash the spinach well and cook for 8–10 minutes in the water adhering to the leaves. Drain well and chop on a plate. Sprinkle with a little grated nutmeg. Shell the hard-boiled eggs, chop the whites and press the yolks through a sieve. Mix the dressing in a good-sized bowl, add the spinach and egg whites and stir. Sprinkle with the sieved egg yolks.

Chicory Salad with Orange

Serves 4–6

This is a refreshing winter salad. If the oranges are very thin skinned I sometimes leave the skin on.

1 or 2 heads chicory
2 ripe oranges, seedless if possible
French Dressing (see p. 105)

Wash and trim the chicory. Cut the leaves in half across if very long. Peel the oranges, if you wish, and slice very thinly. Arrange the chicory and orange slices in a dish and pour the dressing over. This salad will keep well for about 2 hours if kept cool.

Green Salad

Serves 4–6

This is the hardest salad to get just right — the great thing is to have a variety of greenstuff, so that the salad looks interesting as well as giving a range of flavours. All the ingredients must be really fresh. For a lettuce-based green salad it must be a good variety, not the insipid floppy cabbage type sold in millions but a crisp firm lettuce like Webb's Wonderful or Winter Density. It's very difficult to buy a good lettuce, since a lettuce needs just-picked freshness to taste of anything. It's often better to forget lettuce unless you have your own in the garden and use watercress, young spinach leaves, endive or even a blanched dandelion. (Forget that the French name is *pissenlit*!) Simply cover a dandelion with an upturned flowerpot for 7–10 days and, hey presto, you have a delicious salad vegetable for very little trouble — I bet you didn't even have to plant it!

a bowl of lettuce, dandelion or young spinach leaves
a bunch of watercress

½ cucumber and/or a small green pepper, chopped
2–3 spring onions or tops of shallots, chopped
fresh herbs, finely chopped
1 clove garlic
Sauce Vinaigrette or French Dressing (see p. 105)

Wash and drain the lettuce, dandelion, watercress or any other salad vegetable used. Chop the cucumber, green pepper and onions. Arrange all the prepared vegetables in a salad bowl or in individual dishes. Crush the garlic and add to the prepared dressing. Pour over the salad just before serving and sprinkle with the fresh herbs. If the salad is to travel, cover the bowl or dishes with plastic film and chill before packing in an insulated box. Pack the dressing separately so that it can be poured over the salad at the last moment.

Red Cabbage Salad

Serves 4–6

The slightly orangey flavour of coriander gives this quick and easy red cabbage salad a delicate flavour.

¼ pint (150 ml) red wine
2 tablespoons red wine vinegar
½ small red cabbage, shredded
2 Cox's Orange apples, cored and diced
1 tablespoon coriander seeds, bruised
salt and pepper
chopped parsley

Heat the red wine with the vinegar in a saucepan, bring to the boil and tip in the shredded red cabbage and diced apples. Bring back to the boil and simmer fast for 5 minutes. Tip into a bowl, stir in the bruised coriander seeds, salt and freshly milled pepper and allow to cool. Sprinkle with chopped parsley.

White Cabbage Salad

Serves 4

Rather than sauerkraut, which can be too tart for children, I make a cabbage salad with a soured cream dressing.

½ small white cabbage, shredded
½ onion, finely chopped
1 teaspoon caraway seeds
Soured Cream or Yoghurt Dressing (see pp. 107, 108)

Finely shred the cabbage into a bowl. Mix in the chopped onion and sprinkle with the caraway seeds. Pour the dressing over and leave for at least 3–4 hours before serving.

Ratatouille

Serves 4–6

Cool, aromatic Ratatouille on a hot summer's evening is a perfect start to a picnic in the garden, on the patio or the beach.

1 large or 2 medium aubergines
2–3 courgettes
2–3 tomatoes, large if possible
1 large green pepper
1 smaller red pepper
1 large onion
1–2 cloves garlic
4 tablespoons fruity olive oil
1 teaspoon coriander seeds, bruised
salt and pepper
1 tablespoon fresh chopped basil

Slice the aubergines and courgettes, sprinkle with salt and put in a colander with a weighted plate on top so that excess moisture can drip out for about an hour. Skin the tomatoes by immersing them in nearly boiling water. Nick the skins, leave for 1 minute, lift out and then peel and slice. Cut the deseeded peppers in narrow strips. Slice the onion and chop the garlic. Heat the oil in a saucepan or casserole and soften the onion and garlic in it. Then add all the aubergines, peppers and courgettes, cover and simmer very gently for 30 minutes. Add the tomatoes, crushed coriander seeds, some salt and freshly milled black pepper. Cover and simmer for a further 20–30 minutes. Stir in the chopped basil and cool in a pottery dish.

Les Crudités Avec L'Aïoli *Serves 4–6*

This hors d'oeuvre is often to be seen on French restaurant menus. It is simply raw vegetables cut into digestible match-sticks, served with a garlic mayonnaise. It is a refreshing idea for a packed lunch if the vegetables can be kept cool in an icebox. The aioli is served at normal temperature.

a handful of baby French beans or haricot verts
2 carrots
2 sticks celery
a handful of firm mushrooms
4–6 spring onions, trimmed
$\frac{1}{2}$ cucumber
tomatoes, if you wish
$\frac{1}{4}$–$\frac{1}{2}$ pint (150–275 ml) Aïoli (see p. 107)

Blanch the beans for hardly a minute and cool under cold water. Cut the carrots and celery into matchsticks. Slice the mush-rooms downwards and dice the cucumber or cut into match-sticks. Peel and cut the tomatoes into sections. The various components (use whatever other vegetables you have avail-able, e.g. cauliflower, courgettes) should be arranged in little heaps around the aioli, which can be in a pretty pottery dish, and not mixed together in a jumble. In this way the dish looks inviting and the flavours remain distinct.

Mushrooms à la Grecque

Serves 4

This mushroom dish is to be seen in most charcuteries in France. It is a very aromatic hors d'oeuvre which improves overnight.

8 oz (225 g) firm button mushrooms
1 small onion, finely chopped
1 clove garlic, crushed
1½ tablespoons olive oil
2¼ oz (65 g) tin tomato purée
2 tins dry white wine, using tomato purée tin as measure
salt and pepper

Wipe the mushrooms and slice downwards including the stalks. Melt the onion and garlic in the olive oil until soft and transparent. Stir in the tomato purée and twice the amount of white wine. Bring to the boil, season with salt and pepper and add the mushrooms. Simmer for 5–8 minutes. Lift out the mushrooms and simmer the sauce until thick. Pour over the mushrooms and set aside to cool.

Avocado and Prawn Salad

Serves 4

Just the kind of salad for a picnic at the races.

2 ripe avocado pears
juice of ½ lemon
chopped chives
chopped parsley
4 oz (115 g) peeled prawns
Soured Cream Dressing (see p. 108)

Peel and stone the avocado pears. Cut the flesh into ½ in (1 cm) cubes into a shallow dish. Immediately pour the lemon juice over the avocados and gently mix to distribute evenly. Sprinkle with the chopped herbs, arrange the prawns in the middle of the dish and spoon the dressing over them. Alternatively gently toss all the ingredients together and then sprinkle with the herbs.

Endive with Blue Cheese Salad   *Serves 4–6*

In France our kind of lettuce is rarely seen — the crisp slightly bitter endive is much preferred. Endive travels much better than lettuce but does need less vinegar in the dressing. I often use just olive oil and a squeeze of lemon juice.

1 good-sized, curly-leaved endive
1–2 oz (30–55 g) Danish blue cheese
2 oz (55 g) broken walnuts, chopped
1 clove garlic
Sauce Vinaigrette (see p. 105) or just olive oil

Trim the stem from the endive and soak the leaves in very cold water for about an hour (unless you have just cut your endive). Drain the leaves in a wire basket and then dry them in a cloth. Cut the cheese into small dice and chop the walnuts. Rub the bowl with the garlic or crush it into the dressing. Arrange the endive leaves in the bowl, tearing the larger ones into pieces if necessary. Add the cheese and walnuts, pour over the dressing and gently toss until the leaves are well coated. Leave for about 15 minutes before serving.

Salade Niçoise   *Serves 4–6*

One of the most famous of French salads, served as a separate course in France, it is excellent as part of a travelling meal.

1 clove garlic
Sauce Vinaigrette (see p. 105)
1 crisp lettuce, quartered
2 cooked potatoes, diced
4 oz (115 g) cooked French beans, chopped

2 hard-boiled eggs, quartered
3 firm tomatoes, quartered
8 anchovy fillets or 1¾ oz (50 g) tin
7 oz (200 g) tin tuna fish
1 dozen black olives
1 teaspoon capers

Peel and chop or crush the garlic and mix into the dressing. Into a bowl (I prefer a shallow dish if not travelling far, so that the salad is in a mound) put the lettuce, potatoes and beans. Arrange the eggs, tomatoes, anchovies and roughly-flaked tuna fish on top and scatter the olives. Pour the dressing over just before serving and sprinkle with the capers.

Rice Salad with Celery, Apple and Walnuts
Serves 4

Rice salads are delicious; this one is popular with children and I frequently use it as a packed lunch salad. The most important aspect of a rice salad is that the dressing is added when the rice is warm, so that it absorbs the flavour well. This also prevents the rice sticking together in an unappetising way. Rice salads are excellent as travelling food. Try them with different kinds of rice and brown and polished grains and with various dressings. It's hard to beat rice with an oily sauce vinaigrette, but a soured cream dressing works well too.

8 oz (225 g) freshly cooked long grain rice (see p. 136)
2 sticks celery, chopped
2 eating apples, diced
a handful of broken walnuts, chopped
Sauce Vinaigrette or French Dressing (see p. 105)

While the rice is cooking chop the celery and dice the apples, leaving the skin on, and chop the walnuts. Mix the vegetables and nuts with one-third of the dressing. Turn the hot cooked rice into the bowl, pour over the rest of the dressing and stir with a fork. When cool add the rest of the ingredients and leave for at least 30 minutes before serving. This salad is also good with the addition of diced crisp bacon or ham.

Haricot Bean and Tuna Salad   *Serves 4–6*

Some of the most nutritious and sustaining salads use pulses; this bean and fish salad can be a complete meal if necessary.

8 oz (225 g) haricot beans
1 pint (570 ml) stock
1 clove garlic
tarragon or thyme
Sauce Vinaigrette or French Dressing (see p. 105)
2–3 spring onions or shallot tops
1 tablespoon parsley, chopped
7 oz (198 g) tin tuna fish
2–3 slices garlic sausage, diced

Soak the haricot beans in cold water overnight. Next day rinse in clear water and drain. Bring to the boil in the stock with the halved clove of garlic and sprig of tarragon or thyme. Cover and simmer over very low heat or in a moderate oven for $1\frac{1}{2}$–2 hours until the beans are tender. Drain and turn into a pottery dish or bowl. Pour the dressing over, mix in the finely chopped spring onions and parsley and leave to cool. Then stir in the drained, flaked tuna fish and the diced garlic sausage.

Leek Salad with Bacon

Serves 4

When tomatoes are expensive and taste of nothing and lettuces are forced I enjoy making salads from winter vegetables and this is one of my favourites.

1 lb (450 g) leeks, the smaller the better
1 clove garlic
4 rashers smoked streaky bacon
Sauce Vinaigrette or French Dressing (see p. 105)

Peel, trim and wash the leeks. Keep back an inch or so of the green top and chop very finely; cut the rest of the leeks into 1 in (2.5 cm) lengths. Blanch in boiling salted water for 3–4 minutes to just soften the leeks. Drain well (reserve the liquor for soup) and set aside to cool. Chop the peeled garlic and mix with the bacon. Fry or grill the bacon until crisp, then cut into $\frac{1}{2}$ in (1 cm) pieces. Mix the leeks with the bacon and pour the dressing over. Leave to steep for 2 hours so that the leeks absorb the dressing.

Jerusalem Artichoke and Olive Salad *Serves 4*

The smoky flavour of Jerusalem artichokes combines well with olives, especially black ones that have been steeped in brine with plenty of Mediterranean herbs.

1 lb (450 g) Jerusalem artichokes
1 clove garlic (optional)
2–3 tablespoons olives, black or stuffed green
French Dressing (see p. 105)

Scrub the artichokes and cook in boiling salted water until just tender: 8–10 minutes for newly dug artichokes, older ones will need up to 20 minutes. Drain and peel away the skin. Slice the artichokes into a bowl or dish. Add the finely chopped garlic, if you like it, with the stoned olives. Pour the dressing over and allow to cool before serving.

120

Chicken Salad with Celery and Pineapple
Serves 3–4

For a packed lunch in the summer this beats cheese sandwiches in a black briefcase.

1 clove garlic
12 oz (340 g) cooked chicken
1 small head celery, chopped
7 oz (200 g) tin unsweetened pineapple chunks *or* $\frac{1}{4}$ fresh pineapple
chopped parsley
Soured Cream or Yoghurt Dressing (see pp. 107, 108)

Rub the salad bowl with the clove of garlic. Dice the chicken and turn into the bowl with the chopped celery and pineapple chunks. Pour the dressing over and mix. Sprinkle generously with chopped parsley. Chill before serving. This salad is also good with prawns instead of chicken.

Wilma's Potato Salad
Serves 4–6

My father felt that only potatoes were the rightful accompaniment to meat; rice and pasta just didn't suffice. For family picnics in the summer this was my mother's potato salad.

1 lb (450 g) waxy potatoes, King Edward or Desirée
2–3 spring onions or shallots, chopped
Canadian Cooked Salad Dressing (see p. 109)

Scrub the potatoes and cook them in salted water for 15–20 minutes, depending upon size. Drain and as soon as possible peel away the skins. Dice the potatoes into a bowl, sprinkle with the chopped onions and pour over the dressing. Mix gently to coat the potatoes and set aside to cool. Travels splendidly.

Red Kidney Bean Salad with Sweetcorn

Serves 4–6

The colours of this salad look dramatic; it's a very filling salad, ideal after a day's hiking.

8 oz (225 g) dried red kidney beans
bouquet garni, fresh or dried
1 clove garlic
salt
Sauce Vinaigrette or French Dressing (see p. 105)
2–3 spring onions
1 tablespoon chopped parsley
1 tablespoon chopped mint
4–6 oz (115-170 g) frozen sweetcorn

Soak the red kidney beans overnight. Next day refresh in cold water and boil with the bouquet garni and chopped garlic in salted water for 10 minutes, then simmer for about 1 hour or more until the beans are tender. Drain and discard the herbs and garlic and turn into a lidded container. Pour the dressing over straight away and mix in the chopped spring onions, herbs and sweetcorn and leave to cool. In an emergency this salad could be made with tinned red kidney beans and tinned sweetcorn but it won't have the same texture.

Green Lentil Salad with Cervalat

Serves 4

I like to use green lentils for this salad but try it with yellow or brown ones, if you have them.

8 oz (225 g) green lentils
salt
bouquet garni, fresh or dried
2 spring onions or 1 small onion

2 tomatoes, peeled
3–4 oz (85–115 g) German cervalat sausage
1 clove garlic
French Dressing (see p. 105)

Cook the lentils in simmering water with some salt and a bouquet garni over a low heat for about 1 hour. Don't let the lentils
overcook and become mushy. Chop the onions and tomatoes
and dice the cervalat. Crush the garlic and mix with the French
dressing. Drain the lentils, turn into a pottery dish and pour the
dressing over. Gently mix in the onions, tomatoes and cervalat
and leave to cool.

Spiced Rice Salad with Almonds and Raisins
Serves 4

A cousin who has been living in the Middle East showed me
how to make this rice salad — it's delicious served hot or cold.

1 oz (30 g) flaked almonds
2 tablespoons olive oil
1 small onion, finely chopped
1 teaspoon turmeric
1 teaspoon ground cinammon
French Dressing (see p. 105)
8 oz (225 g) hot, cooked rice (see p. 136)
2 oz (55 g) seedless raisins

Toast the almonds under a grill. Heat the olive oil in a frying pan
and quickly fry the almonds for 2 minutes, then lift out on to a
plate. Fry the onion in the oil for 3–4 minutes until golden. Stir in
the turmeric and cinammon and cook together for 2 minutes.
Remove from heat and add to the dressing. Pour over the hot
rice, add the almonds and raisins and mix. Either serve straight
away or pack in an insulated container or leave for 2 hours to
cool.

Smoked Ham and Pasta Salad   *Serves 4*

Pasta needs dressing straight after cooking so that it absorbs the full flavour of the salad. This salad travels perfectly and provides a refreshing change during a long hot summer.

8 oz (225 g) shell pasta or bows
salt
1 teaspoon olive oil
2 cloves garlic, finely sliced
3–4 oz (85–115 g) smoked ham (Polish is good)
fresh basil or marjoram, chopped
1 green pepper
Sauce Vinaigrette or French Dressing (see p. 105)

Cook the pasta in boiling salted water with the oil and one clove of garlic for 8–12 minutes until just tender — *al dente.* Cut the smoked ham in strips and chop the basil or marjoram finely. Cut the green pepper in half and deseed it, then cut into dice and blanch in hot water for 1 minute. Crush the other clove of garlic and mix into the salad dressing. Drain the pasta, turn into a pottery bowl and pour the dressing over straight away. Mix in the ham, herbs and green pepper and leave to cool.

Dried Fruit and Nut Salad   *Serves 4–6*

I invariably add a handful of chopped nuts and some raisins to any salad for children and this salad is made entirely of that. Do add crisp vegetables or fresh fruit to give other variations at times. A very good packed lunch salad, in a small lidded plastic container with a spoon.

12 oz (340 g) dried fruit which may include any or all of the following: raisins, sultanas, dates, dried peaches, dried apricots, prunes, dried bananas, dried apple rings, dried pears
the juice from 2 oranges or 1 glass orange juice

124

4 oz (115 g) mixed chopped nuts, e.g. walnuts, cashews
Cream Cheese or Yoghurt Dressing (see pp. 107, 108)
a little honey if needed

Use kitchen scissors to cut up the dried fruit into smaller pieces, removing stalks and stones. Leave the vine fruits whole. Soak in the orange juice overnight. Next day add the chopped nuts and pour the dressing over. Mix well and add a teaspoon of clear honey if needed.

Well~Tempered
Travelling Dishes

This chapter is about food which will keep hot without complaining; food that will reheat without loss of flavour or texture — in fact some of these dishes actually improve with keeping; and some cold food that can be made well ahead.

Whether you are planning a winter picnic, or visiting a starving student in his garret and are keen to take him a good hot meal that can be reheated on a gas ring, or just reckoning to spend a whole day on the allotment, this is the kind of food for when the weather is cold and a mug of hot soup is not enough.

Much of this food is good farmhouse fare from all over the world. After all, a goulash improves while the goats are milked, rabbit with prunes waits patiently during a calving crisis and shepherd's pie explains all. Try your own favourite casseroled dishes and discover how good-tempered they are as well.

Chicken with Paprika and Cummin *Serves 4*

An excellent dish for an outdoor picnic.

1 tablespoon olive oil
1 tablespoon butter
4 chicken joints, boned preferably
1 medium onion, chopped
1 tablespoon flour
1 tablespoon sweet paprika
1 teaspoon cummin seed, crushed or ground
salt and pepper
14 oz (400 g) tin tomatoes
1 red pimento, fresh or tinned
¼ pint (150 ml) natural yoghurt
1 tablespoon finely chopped parsley

Melt the oil and butter and sear the chicken in it. Remove to a hot casserole and gently cook the onion in the oil until golden and transparent. Stir in the flour, paprika and crushed cummin seed with some salt and milled black pepper, cook together for 1–2 minutes, then pour in the tomatoes and stir over moderate heat until the sauce thickens. Pour over the chicken and cook in a moderate oven, 350°F (180°C), Gas Mark 4, for 45 minutes, or return the joints to the sauce and cook them covered on top of the stove for about 35 minutes. Then stir in the chopped red pimento, spoon the yoghurt over the chicken and strew with chopped parsley. For travelling, pack the chicken in its sauce in a heatproof container and add the yoghurt and parsley just before serving with rice (see p. 136).

GHTF–5

Chilli Con Carne

Good at any time of the year, this dish works well late on a summer's evening in the garden.

1½ lb (680 g) shin of beef
2 tablespoons olive oil
1 medium onion, finely chopped
1–2 cloves garlic, chopped
1 fresh green chilli, chopped
1 tablespoon flour
14 oz (400 g) tin tomatoes
½ teaspoon crushed cummin seed
½ teaspoon oregano
½–1 teaspoon chilli powder
2 bay leaves
salt and pepper
1 lb (450 g) tinned red kidney beans or ½ lb dried, soaked overnight
1 green pepper, deseeded and sliced
2–3 sprigs marjoram, chopped

Trim the meat and cut into 1 in (2.5 cm) cubes. Heat the oil and sear the meat in it. Add the onion, garlic and chilli and stir over medium heat until golden. Stir in the flour and cook for 1–2 minutes; add the tomatoes, cummin, oregano, chilli powder and bay leaves with some salt and freshly milled pepper. Cover and lower the heat or cook in a moderate oven, 350°F (180°C), Gas Mark 4, for 1½ hours. Add the drained kidney beans and the green pepper and cook for a further half an hour. If using dried kidney beans, boil them on their own in plenty of water for 1 hour before adding them, drained, to the dish and then cook for 1 hour. Add the chopped marjoram just before serving with rice (see p. 136).

Boston Pork'n'Beans

Serves 6

An old-fashioned casserole from the east coast of America.

12 oz (340 g) white haricot beans
1 lb (450 g) belly pork
salt and pepper
2 tablespoons molasses
2 teaspoons dry mustard
1 teaspoon salt
14 oz (400 g) tin tomatoes, sieved

Rinse the beans in cold water, then put them in a saucepan with 3 pints (1¾ litres) of cold water. Bring to the boil, remove from heat, cover the saucepan and leave to soak for 40 minutes. Skin the belly pork and remove any bones. Cut the pork into cubes and sprinkle with salt and pepper. Mix the molasses, mustard, salt and sieved tomatoes. Drain the beans and rinse in warm water. Put half the beans in the bottom of a deep earthenware pot. Make a layer of the pork, cover with the rest of the beans and pour over the molasses mixture. Top up with hot water if the liquid is not level with the surface of the beans. If you have a continuously burning cooker cook the dish overnight in the slow oven or in a very slow oven, 275°F (140°C), Gas Mark 1, for 6–8 hours. Check occasionally to see that the dish is not drying up and add a little water if necessary. Stir before serving. This dish keeps hot well and reheats splendidly.

Rabbit with Prunes

Serves 4

We are lucky enough to have local rabbit and cider for this dish.

1 rabbit
½ pint (275 ml) dry cider

1 tablespoon cider or wine vinegar
12 allspice berries, crushed
bouquet of fresh herbs
1 onion or leek
1 carrot or stick of celery
8 oz (225 g) large prunes
3 bay leaves
1 tablespoon flour
salt and pepper
2–3 tablespoons olive oil
1 oz (30 g) butter

Joint the rabbit with a very sharp knife. Marinate overnight in the cider and vinegar with the allspice berries, herbs and sliced vegetables. Soak the prunes overnight in 1 pint (570 ml) of water with the bay leaves. Next day simmer the prunes until soft enough for the stones to be removed and then set the prunes aside. Mix the flour with some salt and freshly milled black pepper in a plastic bag. Lift the rabbit joints from the marinade, drain them well and coat each with flour in the bag. Heat the oil and butter in a pan and brown the rabbit joints; remove to a warm casserole. Pour the marinade into the pan, allow to bubble and pour over the rabbit. Cover the casserole and cook in a moderate oven, 350°F (180°C), Gas Mark 4, for 45 minutes. Add the prunes and cook for a further 30 minutes. Remove the bouquet of herbs, bone the meat if you wish, and bring back to heat. Serve with scalloped potatoes.

SCALLOPED POTATOES
Layer 1 lb (450 g) sliced peeled potatoes and onion in a buttered casserole, seasoning as you do it. Sprinkle with a little flour, a good lump of butter and pour over ½ teacup (3 fl oz/75 ml) of cream or milk. Cook, covered, in a moderate oven for an hour.

Frikadeller Med Rödkaal

Serves 4

I have spent a lot of time at cold country auction sales and it's often the thought of a hot meal like this waiting for me in the car that persuades me not to stay for the next lot! These Danish meatballs with red cabbage wait wonderfully.

1 small or ½ large red cabbage
2 oranges, peeled and sliced
1 oz (30 g) butter
1 clove garlic, sliced
salt and pepper

Meatballs:
8 oz (225 g) best finely minced beef
8 oz (225 g) minced or ground pork
1 small onion, grated
1 egg
½ pint (275 ml) milk
4 oz (115 g) plain flour
½ teaspoon ground cloves
salt and pepper
2–3 tablespoons olive oil
knob of butter

Make the cabbage first. Remove the damaged leaves from the cabbage and shred, discarding the stalk. Peel and slice the oranges. Melt the butter in a flameproof casserole or a heavy-based saucepan and add the sliced garlic. After a few moments add the cabbage, stir to coat with butter and add the orange with some salt and pepper. Cover and cook in a moderate oven, 350°F (180°C), Gas Mark 4, for 45–60 minutes or on a low heat on the stove. While it is cooking, mix the meats together and add the grated onion. Beat the egg and milk together and gradually incorporate the flour and cloves to give a thin batter. Season with salt and pepper, pour on to the meats and mix well. Take dessertspoonfuls and form them into balls in your hands.

Fry in the oil and butter until browned and cook for about 5 minutes. Add to the cooked red cabbage and keep hot in a hay box.

Wurstsuppe

Serves 4–6

This is the midday meal in German farmhouses when it's baking day. It is a nourishing dish of vegetables and sausage, served with dumplings or bread, and eaten with a spoon from large bowls.

4 oz (115 g) white haricot beans
1 onion, diced
1 carrot, diced
1 stick of celery, chopped
1–2 bratwurst
1–2 mettwurst or other smoked pork sausage
⅓ small white cabbage, sliced and chopped
1 large tomato, diced
few French beans, chopped
6–8 Frankfurter sausages
salt and pepper
8 oz (225 g) self-raising flour
finely chopped thyme, fresh or dried
2 oz (55 g) butter, softened
milk to mix

Cover the beans with cold water and bring to the boil. Remove from heat, cover the saucepan and leave for 40 minutes. Drain the beans (outside if you can) and rinse with fresh water. Cover with tepid water and simmer for about 1 hour until nearly tender. Add the onion, carrot and celery and the bratwurst, left whole, and simmer for half an hour. Then add the mettwurst, cut into chunks, with the cabbage, tomato, beans, Frankfurters and some pepper and a little salt, if needed. Bring back to the boil and simmer for 5 minutes. Mix the flour, salt, pepper and chopped thyme together. Cut in the softened butter and mix to a soft dough with some milk. Drop teaspoons of the dough into the simmering soup and cook for 5–8 minutes. Then serve in deep bowls. For serving on a picnic, pack the cooked soup and the dumpling dough separately and cook the dumplings in the simmering soup over a gas picnic stove just before serving.

Carbonnade Flamande

Serves 4–6

This Flemish beef in beer casserole really does improve with keeping.

$1\frac{1}{2}$ lb (680 g) chuck steak or shin of beef
dripping
2 medium onions, finely sliced
1 clove garlic, crushed
1 tablespoon flour
$\frac{1}{2}$ pint (275 ml) brown ale or stout, plus a little extra
1 tablespoon chopped fresh thyme or $\frac{1}{2}$ teaspoon dried
2 bay leaves
salt and pepper
1 tablespoon mustard with seeds, plus a little extra

Cut the beef into 1 in (2.5 cm) cubes, discarding any gristle or fat. Brown the meat in the dripping in the base of a flameproof casserole or a heavy-based saucepan. Lift out the meat with a slotted spoon and keep hot on a plate. Cook the onions and garlic in the rest of the fat until transparent. Add the flour, stir and cook for 1 minute. Gradually add the beer, stirring all the time until the mixture thickens. Return the beef to the casserole, add the thyme and bay leaves with the salt, pepper and mustard. Cover and cook in a slow oven, 325°F (160°C), Gas Mark 3, for $2\frac{1}{2}$–3 hours. Just before serving check the seasoning and add a little more mustard and beer to freshen the flavour. We like this dish with a purée of Jerusalem artichokes and potatoes.

Beef or Lamb Curry

Serves 4–6

Curries always improve with reheating. Beef or lamb works well but you could use chicken too. If so, cook it for less time.

1½ lb (680 g) trimmed lean stewing beef or lamb
1 tablespoon dripping or oil
1 large onion, chopped
1 clove garlic, finely sliced or crushed
1 rounded dessertspoon curry paste (or according to taste)
1 teaspoon garam masala
1 teaspoon caraway seeds
1 large apple, peeled and chopped
1 tablespoon marmalade
14 oz (400 g) tin tomatoes

Cut the beef or lamb into 1 in (2.5 cm) pieces. Melt the dripping in a flameproof casserole or heavy-based saucepan and cook the onion and garlic for 8–10 minutes over low heat until they are golden and transparent. Add the curry paste and stir to cook gently for 2–3 minutes. Tip in the beef and stir to coat the meat. Add the garam masala, caraway seeds, apple, marmalade and tomatoes. Bring to the boil, stir and cover. Cook over low heat or in a slow oven at 325°F (160°C), Gas Mark 3, for about 1½ hours until the meat is tender. Allow to cool and reheat before serving with plain boiled rice and chutney.

Perfect Boiled Rice

Serves 2–3

This method for cooking rice is based on one of Len Deighton's excellent cookstrips from the *Observer* in the Sixties. It never fails, and provides perfectly boiled rice with a good flavour. It is delicious served hot or tossed in an oil and lemon juice dressing when warm as the basis for a rice salad to be served cold.

1 large mug Patna rice
1 large mug cold water

1 small onion, chopped
6 cloves
2 bay leaves
1 tablespoon olive oil
salt and pepper

Measure the rice and tip it into a nylon sieve. Hold it under the cold tap and let the water wash over the rice until it runs clear from the sieve; this takes 2–4 minutes depending on the amount of rice. This thorough washing is the secret of this recipe. Now tip the rice into a heavy-based saucepan with the mug of water, onion, cloves, bay leaves, oil, salt and pepper. Bring the rice to the boil. Immediately turn the heat to the lowest setting possible, stir once and cover with a tight-fitting lid. Now time the rice for 17 minutes exactly. Turn off the heat and leave covered for 5 minutes before serving. The rice will be perfectly cooked with separate grains, none will adhere to the saucepan, nor will the rice need drying out in the oven.

I find rice cooked this way keeps in remarkably good condition packed in a pre-warmed, wide-necked insulated flask for travelling.

Lamb Chops Boulangère   *Serves 4–6*

A French hot-pot which is very sustaining in the winter.

4–6 lamb chops, loin or chump
salt and pepper
knob of butter
1½–2 lb (680–900 g) potatoes, peeled and sliced
½ lb (225 g) onions, sliced
fresh thyme, chopped
¼ pint (150 ml) stock or water

Trim the meat free of all surplus fat and season with salt and pepper. Butter a casserole and make a layer of potatoes and

137

onions in the base; sprinkle with salt and pepper. Cover with the chops, sprinkle with chopped thyme and layer the rest of the potatoes and onions on top. Pour over the stock or water. Cover and cook in a slow oven, 300°F (150°C), Gas Mark 2, for 2 hours. Wrap in a blanket or soft cloth and pack in a hay box or insulated container.

Hungarian Goulash

Serves 4–6

I prefer a strong peppery paprika for goulash; the yoghurt is then an excellent foil.

1½ lb (680 g) chuck steak
2 tablespoons beef dripping
2 onions, sliced
1 clove garlic, crushed
1 tablespoon strong paprika
1 tablespoon flour
14 oz (400 g) tin tomatoes
2 teaspoons caraway seeds
salt and pepper
1 green pepper, seeded and chopped
5 fl oz (150 ml) natural yoghurt

Trim the chuck steak and cut into 1 in (2.5 cm) pieces. In a flameproof casserole or saucepan brown the beef in the melted dripping then lift out the meat with a slotted spoon and keep hot. Soften the onions and garlic in the rest of the dripping and stir in the paprika and flour. Cook together for 2 minutes and then add the tomatoes, caraway seeds, salt and pepper. Stir and cook until a sauce is formed, return the meat to the casserole, cover and cook over moderate heat or in a slow oven, 325°F (160°C), Gas Mark 3, for about 1¾ hours until the meat is tender. Add the chopped green pepper and cook for a further 10 minutes. Spoon the yoghurt over just before serving. Noodles or rice go well with goulash.

Small Shepherd's Pies   *Makes 4 large or 8 small*

These are not just for small shepherds, although I've yet to
discover a child who didn't enjoy easy-to-eat shepherd's pie,
especially if made and served in its own dish. I use oval
earthenware pie dishes, either my own or Mason's Ironstone,
Size 1 for children, Size 2 or 3 for adults. I prefer to start with raw
meat. I usually mince chuck steak at home or use good-quality
minced meat with very little fat. If you wish to use already
cooked meat follow the recipe but omit the 50–60 minute
cooking and go straight on to the potato covering.

1 lb (450 g) minced beef or lamb
salt and pepper
2–3 tablespoons olive oil or dripping
1 onion, chopped
1 clove garlic, chopped (optional)
14 oz (400 g) tin tomatoes
2 carrots, grated
1 tablespoon chopped fresh herbs, especially thyme
2 drops Tabasco or soy sauce
small knob butter
2 teaspoons flour
1½ lb (680 g) potatoes
¼ pint (150 ml) hot milk
2 oz (55 g) butter
salt and pepper

Start by mixing plenty of salt and freshly milled black pepper
into the meat. Heat the oil or dripping in a pan and cook the
onion and garlic until soft but still golden. Add the meat and stir
fry until the meat is no longer red. Tip in the tomatoes, grated
carrot and herbs, plus Tabasco or soy sauce, if liked. Stir
together, breaking up the tomatoes as you do so. Cover the pan
and turn the heat to the lowest setting so that the meat cooks
very gently for 50–60 minutes. Work the softened butter and
flour together on a plate, add to the meat mixture in small pieces

and stir until it thickens. Pour the mixture into individual pie dishes until half full. To make perfect creamed potatoes, cook the scrubbed potatoes in boiling salted water for 12–17 minutes, depending upon variety and size. Drain and peel the potatoes and put them through a mouli-légumes on finest sieve, or mash with a potato masher (it's hard to get the mixture so smooth, though). Add the hot milk and butter. Mix well and season with plenty of black pepper. Spoon over the meat and, using a fork, mark the surface with wavy lines. Bake in a moderate oven at 375°F (190°C), Gas Mark 5, for 25 minutes until golden brown, or brown under a grill.

Picnic Parcels

Anything cooked *en papillote* in a parcel of buttered paper or, more easily, aluminium foil is an exciting surprise. I like this method for outdoor eating because the food stays so hot in its wrapping and the method favours endless combinations of flavours. Simply seasoned with salt, pepper, some fresh herbs and a lump of butter the food cooks in its own juices. This is also a good method for barbecues, providing the meat, fish or vegetables are not cut too thick. Try the same method with bananas sprinkled with brown sugar and lemon juice.

LAMB CHOPS EN PAPILLOTE
lamb chops, thin cut
pepper and salt
new potatoes, scraped and sliced
chopped mint
spring onions, chopped
butter

Trim the lamb chops of fat and lay each on a square of buttered foil. Sprinkle with pepper and salt and add the sliced potatoes, some chopped mint and spring onions. Dot with butter and fold up the foil securely. Either cook in a moderate oven, 350°F (180°C), Gas Mark 4, for 30–40 minutes and transport in a hay box, or cook over a barbecue for 45 minutes.

Meat Loaf Ring

Serves 6–8

A meat loaf cooked in a ring mould is excellent hot with a tomato sauce or cold with the ring filled with a crisp salad and a horseradish and apple sauce.

1 lb (450 g) best minced beef
½ lb (225 g) minced pork or bacon pieces
2 oz (55 g) wholemeal breadcrumbs
6¾ oz (190 g) tin tomatoes
2 egg yolks
1 small onion, finely chopped
1 clove garlic, crushed
3 sticks celery, chopped
1 green pepper, diced
2 tablespoons fresh herbs
1½ teaspoons salt
¼ teaspoon milled black pepper
¼ teaspoon ground allspice

Mix the minced meats with the breadcrumbs, chopped tomatoes and their liquid and the egg yolks. The mixture will be quite wet until the bread has absorbed the liquid. Add the onion, garlic, celery and green pepper with the herbs and seasonings. Spoon into a well-buttered 2-pint (1¼ litres) capacity ring mould and cook in the centre of a moderate oven, 350°F (180°C), Gas Mark 4, for 50–60 minutes. The meat loaf can also be cooked in a 2-pint (1¼ litres) loaf tin and served sliced.

141

Pressed Ox Tongue

I always prepare an ox tongue when I feel that summer has really arrived. This is very good if you have a lot of people to feed; the meat slices beautifully and goes so well with a salad.

1 ox tongue, salted and smoked if possible
1 pig's trotter, cut in half
1 onion, stuck with cloves
1 large carrot, sliced
1 stick celery
bouquet garni of fresh herbs
8 peppercorns

Follow your butcher's instructions for how long to soak the tongue; it will vary from 15 minutes to 24 hours. Cover the tongue with water in a good-sized casserole or use a preserving pan. Slowly bring the water to the boil, and after half an hour taste the water. If it is very salty discard it and start again with cold water. Add the trotter, vegetables, herbs and peppercorns to the water and bring to the boil. Cover and turn down the heat so that the tongue simmers gently, on top of the stove or in a moderate oven, for 3–4 hours, until a sharp knife will go into the meat easily (Mrs. Beeton recommends a straw!). Lift out the tongue and skin it while it is hot, removing any little bones and gristle. Discard the trotter and the vegetables. Reduce the liquor over moderate heat and check it isn't too salty; I often add a little red wine at this stage to give the jelly a good colour. Press the tongue into a straight-sided cake tin or soufflé dish, curling it round as you do so. Pour the liquor over it almost to cover. Put a weighted plate on top so that the meat is pressed down into shape. Leave overnight in a cold place to set. Then remove the plate, wrap a hot dry cloth around the tin or dish and invert to turn out the tongue. Slice thinly across to serve.

Glazed Baked Ham

Home cooked ham is so much more delicious than the bought kind that it is well worth taking the trouble to cook either a piece or a whole gammon now and again — certainly at Christmas. After trying various ways of glazing the gammon over the years, I always return to Elizabeth David's recipe given in *Spices, Salt and Aromatics in the English Kitchen*.

a whole or piece of gammon
1 onion, stuck with cloves
bouquet garni
1–2 tablespoons cloves
2 heaped tablespoons dark soft brown sugar
1 teaspoon made mustard
4 tablespoons milk

Soak the gammon in cold water for up to 24 hours, changing the water 2 or 3 times. Either bake the gammon, wrapped in foil, in a tin half full of water in a slow oven, 325°F (160°C), Gas Mark 3, for 45 minutes to the pound, or bring to the boil in a preserving pan with the cloved onion and bouquet garni in water just to cover, and gently simmer for 30 minutes to the pound. (This way you have a splendid supply of ham stock if the gammon is not too salty.) Remove the meat from the oven or pan and while it is still hot peel away the rind. I usually cut a lattice design into the fat with a sharp knife and stud each diamond with a clove. Place the gammon in a roasting tin. Mix the sugar, mustard and milk and spoon some of it over the meat. Cook for a further 30 minutes at the top of the oven (at the same temperature), basting with the glaze now and again. The gammon will cook to a beautiful golden brown. Set aside to cool and cut the next day.

Spiced Chicken Joints

Serves 4–8

This way of preparing chicken is always popular. I serve the boned breast of chicken to the younger children and adults enjoy eating the legs in the style of Henry VIII.

1–2 jointed chickens, small tender ones are good
1 onion stuck with cloves
1 carrot
1 stick celery
bouquet of fresh herbs
salt and pepper
2 oz (55 g) butter
1 clove garlic, crushed
piece of fresh or preserved ginger, finely chopped
1 teaspoon ground coriander
½ teaspoon cardamom seeds, crushed
2 tablespoons mango chutney or lime marmalade
lemon or lime juice

Joint the chicken with a sharp knife or cook whole and then cut into pieces. Poach the chicken in just enough water to cover with the onion, carrot, celery, herbs and some salt and pepper until tender. Allow to cool in the liquid. Soften the butter and work in the crushed garlic and finely chopped ginger. Add the spices and chutney with a squeeze of lemon or lime juice and some salt and pepper, mix together until soft and spreadable. Arrange the cooled chicken on a heatproof dish, spread each piece of chicken with the spiced butter and allow to get very cold in the fridge. Then brown under a very hot grill until golden and sizzling. Either serve straight away with a crisp salad or serve cold with a rice, nut and apricot salad.

Pork Fillet Kebabs
Serves 6–8

Sometimes it's possible to plan a barbecue at the end of your journey and it does make a marvellous evening picnic. Lamb chops, steaks, spare ribs and hamburgers are all ideal for barbecuing — over charcoal or a wood fire — but my favourite are kebabs. If you transport the meat in its marinade it will be perfect for threading on to skewers just before cooking.

2 or more pork fillets (tenderloin)
3–4 tablespoons olive oil
1–2 cloves garlic, crushed
2 tablespoons finely chopped mint
2 tablespoons finely chopped chives
salt and pepper
6 fresh tomatoes
2–3 fresh green peppers
12 bay leaves, fresh if possible

Trim the meat of any fat and cut across into 2 in (5 cm) cubes. Mix the olive oil with the crushed garlic, herbs and salt and pepper in a flat dish. Add the meat and turn over in the marinade to coat all surfaces. Leave in a cool place for 2–3 hours (or during the journey). When ready to cook the kebabs, quarter or halve the tomatoes, halve and deseed the peppers and cut into pieces. Then start to assemble the kebabs, allowing at least one skewer per person. Thread pieces of meat, tomato and green pepper alternately on to each skewer, distributing the bay leaves between them. Brush with marinade and barbecue the kebabs, turning them now and again to cook the meat evenly. Serve with fresh bread or hot rice and salad.

Jacket Potatoes

At last the potato is regaining its position in the vegetable firmament after the battering it has received from the slimming pundits for the last 20 years. A potato cooked in its 'field clothes', as the French say, is a most nutritious food — sliced in half and covered with some chopped kidney in an aromatic sauce or some creamy cheese with herbs it is a meal in itself. We also find that many of the sandwich fillings (see p. 49), especially those for toasted sandwiches, work well on jacket potatoes. Baked potatoes will keep hot splendidly if wrapped in thick cloth and packed, the more the better, in a hay box or insulated container. Sometimes it is more convenient to fill the potatoes before travelling: simply scoop out the potato flesh, mix with the filling and replace in the skin, sandwich the potatoes together and reheat to make sure they are piping hot before wrapping and packing. I also pack plenty of butter so that those of us who like the skins can cover them with butter first! Now for a brisk walk to use up all that energy . . .

The best potatoes for baking in their jackets are whichever variety you enjoy eating. They must be maincrop potatoes like Desirée, King Edward or Pentland Crown. I find both floury and waxy varieties bake well but the waxy ones usually have a superior taste and may take a little longer to cook. I always choose large flat potatoes which cook more quickly and slice in half better. Simply scrub the tubers well and dry on a clean cloth. Prick all over in 3 or 4 places with a fork to prevent explosions and arrange either on the floor of your oven or on a baking sheet first. I don't rub the skins with oil or salt or wrap the potatoes in foil. I find all these tricks give a potato that doesn't taste so good and also has a limp skin, which is not popular, but if you prefer that, use oil or foil. I usually bake the potatoes in a moderate oven, 350°F (180°C), Gas Mark 4, but they are a very accommodating vegetable and they are always cooked while I am baking some other dish anyway. The most important thing is that they are given enough time — at least $1\frac{1}{2}$ hours and often 2 hours, depending on size — fortunately there is quite a degree of latitude. They are always well received served plain with lots of fresh butter and the pepper and salt mills. But here are some fillings which I have found go down extremely well. Each will fill 6–8 potatoes.

KIDNEYS IN WINE SAUCE
A strongly-flavoured filling that contrasts well with a creamy baked potato.

4–6 lamb's kidneys
1 small onion
1 clove garlic
knob of butter
wine glass of red wine
salt and pepper
1 teaspoon butter blended with 1 teaspoon flour
a little chopped thyme

Skin the kidneys and cut into small pieces, discarding the cores. Chop the onion and garlic finely and cook in the butter in a small pan until soft. Add the kidneys and when they have changed colour pour in the wine. Bubble together for 2 minutes, then season with salt and pepper. Blend the butter with the flour, add to the pan in small pieces and stir together well for 3–4 minutes over moderate heat until the sauce thickens. Sprinkle with chopped thyme and spoon into a dish or lidded insulated container.

COTTAGE CHEESE WITH HERBS AND GARLIC
A very popular filling for jacket potatoes especially in America.

8 oz (225 g) cottage cheese
5 fl oz (142 ml) soured cream (can be omitted for slimmers)
1 clove garlic, crushed
1–2 tablespoons fresh herbs: chives, parsley and mint
salt and pepper

In a bowl combine the cottage cheese, soured cream, crushed garlic and the herbs. Season with salt and pepper. I sometimes add a little barbecue spice or ground cummin too. Spoon into a dish or lidded pot to serve with the jacket potatoes.

BACON AND SWEETCORN FILLING
8 oz (225 g) bacon rashers, smoked streaky is fine
¼ pint (150 ml) creamy milk
2 tablespoons butter
2 tablespoons flour
8 oz (225 g) defrosted or tinned sweetcorn
black pepper

Grill the bacon until crisp and then cut into dice or short lengths. Make a white sauce by simply mixing the milk, butter and flour together fast in a small saucepan over moderate heat until thick. Add the drained sweetcorn and bacon. Season with pepper and a little salt, if necessary. Remove from the heat and spoon into a dish or lidded insulated container.

Stuffed Eggs

A selection of stuffed eggs served with a favourite salad and plenty of crusty bread makes an excellent easy summer picnic for children to prepare.

DEVILLED STUFFED EGGS
6 hard-boiled eggs, boiled for 7–8 minutes
1 oz (30 g) softened butter
1 tablespoon creamy milk
1–2 teaspoons Worcester sauce
1 teaspoon Dijon or other made mustard
3–4 drops Tabasco sauce
salt and pepper
cayenne pepper or chopped chives

148

Soak the cracked hard-boiled eggs in cold water for 5 minutes, then peel away the shells. Cut in half lengthways. Carefully scoop out the yolks into a bowl with a teaspoon. Add the softened butter and milk and work to a paste with a fork. Mix in the Worcester sauce, mustard and Tabasco sauce and season to taste with a little salt and some black pepper. Spoon back into the halved eggs and sprinkle with a little cayenne pepper or chives. For travelling it is sometimes better to sandwich the eggs so that the filling still shows.

ANCHOVY STUFFED EGGS

4 hard-boiled eggs, boiled for 7–8 minutes
1 oz (30 g) softened butter
1¾ oz (50 g) tin anchovy fillets
1 teaspoon Dijon or made mustard
a pinch of cayenne pepper

Prepare the eggs as above until the yolks are removed from the whites. Use a fork to break up the yolks and work in the butter. Rinse the anchovy fillets in a little warm water and chop very finely. Mix the anchovies into the egg yolks gradually with the mustard and some cayenne pepper. Beat the mixture until smooth, then spoon back into the egg halves.

TOMATO AND HERB STUFFED EGGS

4 hard-boiled eggs
1 tablespoon tomato purée
1 oz (30 g) softened butter
¼ teaspoon paprika
salt and pepper
1 tablespoon fresh marjoram or parsley, finely chopped

Prepare the eggs as above until the yolks are in a small bowl. Use a fork to break up the yolks and mix to a paste with the tomato purée, butter and paprika. Season with salt and pepper and add the marjoram or parsley. Spoon back into the egg halves.

Omelettes, Frittatas and Tortillas

Omelettes are not only splendid hot and cooked to order, but they are suprisingly good cold. An Italian frittata or a Spanish tortilla is an omelette that contains vegetables and is cooked on both sides. Served in wedges, all these omelettes are a very good and quickly prepared picnic food.

MUSHROOM OMELETTE   *Serves 1–2*
2 oz (55 g) mushrooms
1 oz (30 g) butter
salt and pepper
coffeespoon of flour
2 tablespoons cream
2–3 eggs
small knob of unsalted butter

Make the mushroom filling first in a small saucepan. Wipe the mushrooms, chop them finely and cook them in the butter until soft. Season with a little salt and pepper and sprinkle with the flour. Cook, stirring, for 1–2 minutes and then add the cream. Cook until thick and then set aside but keep hot. Put a 6 in (15 cm) omelette pan with curved sides to heat slowly. Break the eggs into a bowl, season with salt and pepper and use a fork to lightly beat the yolks into the whites. Drop the butter into the hot pan, tilt to coat the base and just as it starts to colour pour in the egg mixture. Shake the pan so that uncooked mixture runs under the edges, and while the top is still a little runny spoon the mushroom filling into the middle third of the omelette. Flip over the omelette and slide on to a plate. Allow to cool and sandwich between two slices of bread or a Vienna loaf.

SPANISH ONION TORTILLA   *Serves 1–2*
1 Spanish onion, finely sliced
1 tablespoon olive oil
salt and pepper
2–3 eggs

Use a small omelette pan to cook the onion in the olive oil over moderate heat until it is golden and transparent. Sprinkle with salt and pepper. Lightly beat the eggs with a fork with a little salt and pepper. Pour the eggs over the onion and shake the pan to make sure the mixture has spread over the base of the pan. Cook until the top surface is set and quickly flip the tortilla over. When both sides are golden, turn on to a plate and cut into wedges when the tortilla is cold.

COURGETTE AND GREEN PEPPER FRITTATA *Serves 3–4*
When cut into small pieces this is very good for staving off hunger pangs while setting up a picnic.

2–3 baby courgettes, sliced
1 small green pepper, deseeded and chopped
1 tomato, skinned and chopped
1 tablespoon olive oil
1 tablespoon butter
salt and pepper
fresh herbs (optional)
4–6 eggs

Prepare the vegetables and cook them gently in the oil and butter in an 8 in (20 cm) omelette pan. Then season with salt and pepper and some fresh herbs if you wish. Use a fork to break up the eggs in a small basin with a little salt and pepper, and pour on to the vegetables. Shake the pan to make sure the egg has run to the base of the pan. Loosen with a knife if it is sticking. When the surface has set, use two fish slices or a plate to turn over the frittata. Cook until golden underneath, then slide on to a plate and cut into wedges.

Spinach Pancake

Serves 4

An Italian green omelette. I find about 1 lb (450 g) fresh spinach gives the right amount of cooked purée.

½ lb (225 g) cooked spinach purée (about 8 heaped tablespoons)
grated nutmeg
6 eggs
salt and pepper
1 tablespoon finely chopped herbs
olive oil
Parmesan cheese

Wash the spinach and cook in just the water adhering to the leaves; add the salt when the spinach has shrunk. Drain the spinach in a sieve and purée in a liquidiser. Season with freshly grated nutmeg. Break the eggs into a bowl, add salt and pepper, the herbs and the spinach purée. Beat with a fork until well combined. Heat a little olive oil in an omelette pan and pour in mixture to cover the base. Cook over moderate heat until it is golden underneath and the surface is just beginning to set. Sprinkle generously with Parmesan cheese and put under a very hot grill to set the top of the pancake and to melt the cheese. Turn or roll on to a very hot plate to eat straight away or leave to cool and eat with crisp French bread. For travelling, remove a little of the bread and pack the rolled pancakes lengthways in a French or Vienna loaf. As a change some Boursin cheese with garlic is delicious instead of Parmesan.

Puddings

Canadian Raisin Pie, Stuffed Peaches, Frozen Coffee Mousse or a custard tart are all delightful ways of completing a meal. I have chosen puddings that will survive travelling and still taste scrumptious and most of them we eat at home as well.

Canadian Raisin Pie

This is one of my mother's picnic pies — it looks lovely with its lattice pastry top and tastes delicious served hot or cold with pouring cream.

Pastry:
6 oz (170 g) plain flour
1 oz (30 g) vanilla sugar
good pinch of salt
1½ oz (45 g) margarine
1½ oz (45 g) vegetable fat
2–3 tablespoons cold water

Filling:
4 oz (115 g) dark soft brown sugar
2 tablespoons cornflour
½ pint (275 ml) water
10 oz (290 g) seedless raisins
finely grated rind and juice of 1 orange *or* 2 tablespoons rum
1 oz (30 g) unsalted butter
egg yolk or cream for glazing

Sieve the flour, sugar and salt into a bowl. Cut in the fats and rub in until like breadcrumbs. Mix to a dough with the water and set aside to rest. Make the filling by putting all the ingredients into a heavy-based saucepan. Mix well and bring to the boil over medium heat. Cook together for 3–4 minutes until the mixture is thick, clear and glossy. Set aside to cool. Roll out the pastry to ⅛ in (3 mm) thickness and line a greased 8 in (20 cm) shallow pie dish with it. Spoon in the filling and make level. Roll out the pastry trimmings and cut ½ in (1 cm) wide strips with a toothed pasta wheel. Lay 5 strips of pastry across the pie and another 5 strips across those so that a diamond lattice is formed. Gently press the ends of the strips into the pastry pie rim and then crimp the rim. Brush the pastry with the egg yolk or cream. Bake the pie on a baking sheet in the centre of a hot oven at 425°F

(220°C), Gas Mark 7, for 25–30 minutes, until the pastry is crisp and golden.

Apple Pie with Cheese Pastry   *Serves 6–8*

I like to leave a pie in the pantry for my family if I am to be away for a few days. This one is always appreciated, served hot or cold. Cloves go well with the apple but you could try cinammon or nutmeg. A squeeze of lemon juice and some sultanas are good too. Use a coloured cheese in the pastry for a pretty look.

Cheese pastry:
8 oz (225 g) plain flour
pinch salt
2 oz (55 g) margarine
2 oz (55 g) vegetable fat
4 oz (115 g) English cheese such as Cheshire
1 egg yolk
3 tablespoons cold water

Filling:
1½ lb (680 g) cooking apples, e.g. Bramleys
3 oz (85 g) caster sugar
1 tablespoon cornflour
12 cloves (reserve 2 for the top)
milk for glazing

Sieve the flour and salt into a mixing bowl. Rub in the fats and use a knife to mix in the finely grated cheese. Beat the egg yolk with the cold water and mix into the flour to make a soft dough. Line a greased 9 in (23 cm) diameter, 2 in (5 cm) deep pie dish with just over half the pastry. Peel and core the apples and cut into slices. Mix the sugar with the cornflour. Make a layer of apples in the pie dish, sprinkle with half the sugar mixture and half the cloves. Repeat with the rest of the apples, sugar and cloves. Cover the pie with the rest of the pastry. Roll out the pastry trimmings to make two pastry apples (use a clove at the

156

base of each) and some leaves. Brush the pie crust with a little milk and gently press the decoration on top, crimp the pie edge and make 3 or 4 steam vents. Bake in the centre of a hot oven, 425°F (220°C), Gas Mark 7, for 15 minutes, then lower the heat to 350°F (180°C), Gas Mark 4, for a further 30 minutes or until the apples are tender.

Almond Cream Flan   *Serves 6–8*

A delicious French tart.

Pastry:
6 oz (170 g) plain flour
1 oz (30 g) vanilla sugar
3 oz (85 g) unsalted butter
2–3 tablespoons cold water

Filling:
4 oz (115 g) caster sugar
$1\frac{1}{2}$ oz (45 g) ground almonds
$1\frac{1}{2}$ oz (45 g) plain flour
4 egg yolks
$\frac{1}{2}$ pint (275 ml) milk
a few drops almond essence
a little grated lemon rind

Make the pastry by sieving the flour and sugar into a bowl. Rub the butter into the flour until it resembles breadcrumbs. Mix to a dough with the water. Rest the pastry if you have time and then roll out to $\frac{1}{8}$ in (3 mm) thickness on a floured board. Line an 8–9 in (20–23 cm) flan ring or straight-sided shallow pie dish. Mix the sugar, almonds and flour together in a bowl. Beat the egg yolks, milk, almond essence and lemon rind together and pour on to the dry ingredients. Stir well and pour into the pastry case. Bake in the centre of a moderately hot oven at 400°F (200°C), Gas Mark 6, for 25–30 minutes. Allow to cool before cutting and serving.

Coconut Tart

This is such a good firm tart from the Lake District that it is excellent for a packed meal.

Pastry:
6 oz (170 g) plain flour
1½ oz (45 g) margarine
1½ oz (45 g) vegetable fat
2–3 tablespoons cold water

Filling:
2 tablespoons raspberry jam
2 oz (55 g) unsalted butter
1 oz (30 g) caster sugar
1 tablespoon golden syrup
1 egg, beaten
4 oz (115 g) desiccated coconut

Sieve the flour into a bowl and rub the fats in until like bread-crumbs. Mix to a dough with the water. Rest the dough (and yourself!) if you have time. Then roll out on a floured board and line a greased 7 in (18 cm) flan dish. Spread the jam over the pastry base in an even layer. Melt the butter, sugar and syrup in a saucepan over gentle heat. Stir in the egg and coconut and spread over the jam layer. Bake in the centre of a moderate oven, 375°F (190°C), Gas Mark 5, for 25–30 minutes.

Fresh Lemon Tarts

Makes 12

These tarts travel far better than a lemon meringue pie and are beautifully lemony. This recipe will make 12 small tartlets or one tart 8 in (20 cm) across.

Shortcrust pastry:
6 oz (170 g) plain flour
1½ oz (45 g) soft margarine
1½ oz (45 g) vegetable fat
3 tablespoons cold water

Filling:
2 oz (55 g) unsalted butter
juice and grated rind of 2 large lemons
5 oz (140 g) caster sugar
3 large eggs

Make the pastry by rubbing the fats into the flour until the mixture resembles breadcrumbs. Add the water and use a knife to mix to a soft dough. Roll out on a floured board and line 12 greased patty tins or an 8 in (20 cm) flan ring or dish. Very lightly prick the bases of the pastry cases and for the larger tart place a piece of greaseproof paper in the base and cover with butter beans. Bake the pastry cases above the centre of a moderately hot oven, 400°F (200°C), Gas Mark 6, for 7 minutes for the small cases and 10 minutes for the large, remove the paper and beans and bake for a further 2–3 minutes. Remove from the oven and turn the heat down to 350°F (180°C), Gas Mark 4.

To make the filling, pour 1 in (2.5 cm) of boiling water into a saucepan. Fit a bowl over the saucepan and cut the butter into it. Add the eggs and stir in the sugar and the finely grated lemon rind and lemon juice. Stir all together over the just simmering water until the sugar is dissolved. Remove from heat and spoon the filling into the pastry cases. Bake the tarts in the centre of the oven for 18 minutes for the tartlets, 25 minutes for the tart.

Fruit Tartlets

These tartlet cases can be baked ahead and filled at the last moment. Although at their best freshly baked, I find the pastry cases freeze remarkably well. Fill the tarts with any fresh fruit that is in season, poached if necessary, and covered with a slightly thickened sugar syrup.

Pâte sucrée:
4 oz (115 g) plain flour
2 oz (55 g) vanilla sugar
a good pinch salt
2 oz (55 g) unsalted butter
2 eggs yolks

Fresh fruit: strawberries, raspberries, peaches or poached gooseberries, pears or apricots.

Sieve the flour, sugar and salt on to a pastry board or into the bottom of a shallow bowl. Make a well in the centre and cut the butter into it, add the egg yolks and use the fingertips to work all the ingredients together to make a soft paste. You may need to add up to a tablespoon of cold water depending on the flour or the heat of the kitchen. Knead the pastry until smooth and then wrap in a plastic bag and chill for about an hour. Brush melted butter into some tartlet tins; I use round or oval fluted tins. Roll out the pastry to $\frac{1}{8}$ in (3 mm) thickness. Line the tins with the pastry and cut level with the rims. Bake on a baking sheet in a moderate oven, 375°F (190°C), Gas Mark 5, for 15–20 minutes until they are a pale biscuit colour with the rim just darkening a little. Don't let the pastry brown or the flavour will be lost. Cool on the baking sheet and when cold remove the cases from their tins. Fill as required and freeze the others in a lidded plastic container. Makes about 12 tartlets $3\frac{1}{2}$ in (9 cm) across.

Bread Pudding

Serves 8–10

You either love or loathe bread pudding; this version has an interesting texture and an orange flavour.

8 oz (225 g) stale bread, white, wholemeal or mixed
½ pint (275 ml) milk
2 oz (55 g) rolled oats
2 eggs, beaten
2 oz (55 g) dark soft brown sugar
grated rind and juice of a large orange
12 oz (340 g) mixed dried fruit
3 oz (85 g) soft margarine

Break or cut the stale bread into pieces and pour the milk over it. Leave to soak for 30 minutes. If in a hurry turn the bread into crumbs in a liquidiser and mix with the milk. Stir in all the rest of the ingredients and mix together well. Spoon into a well greased cake tin, 8 × 4 in (20 × 10 cm), and make level. Bake in the centre of a slow oven, 325°F (160°C), Gas Mark 3, for 1½ hours. Allow to cool in the tin and then cut into squares.

Russian Pashka

Serves 6–8

This is a scrumptious pudding which I always make at Easter but it is very good at any time of the year. A lovely dish to take to a shared picnic, or a holiday cottage.

4 oz (115 g) unsalted butter
8 oz (225 g) caster sugar (vanilla sugar is best)
2 egg yolks
½ teaspoon vanilla essence
1 lb (450 g) curd cheese
4 oz (115 g) candied peel, chopped
4 oz (115 g) seedless raisins
2 egg whites
a few glacé cherries
a little angelica

161

Cream the butter with half the sugar and when fluffy beat in the egg yolks and vanilla essence (use only a drop if you have used vanilla sugar). Mix in the curd cheese in 2 or 3 amounts. Fold in the candied peel and raisins. Whisk the egg whites until stiff and gradually fold in the rest of the sugar. Use a metal spoon to fold the egg whites into the cheese mixture. Spoon into a pretty bowl or small ramekins and set aside for 3–4 hours at least. Decorate with halved glacé cherries and diamond-shaped pieces of angelica. I've found this pudding will freeze and can be packed frozen and allowed to defrost on the journey.

Plum Clafoutis

Serves 6

This is a great favourite in August when our large and ancient plum tree yields a bountiful supply of juicy dark red plums. This French pudding is also delicious with pears, cherries or apricots served hot or cold. I enjoy it with coffee under a tree on a sunny morning.

1 lb (450 g) plums, cherries or other fresh fruit
3 eggs
2 oz (55 g) caster sugar
pinch of salt
2½ oz (70 g) plain flour
¾ pint (425 ml) creamy milk
1 oz (30 g) butter
1 oz (30 g) vanilla sugar

Cut the plums in half, stone them and arrange in the bottom of a well-buttered fireproof dish. I use an 11 × 6½ in (28 × 18 cm) Pyrex dish. Beat the eggs with the sugar, salt and flour. Warm the milk with the butter until it is just dissolved. Pour on to the egg mixture, beat well and pour over the plums. Bake in the centre of a hot oven, 425°F (220°C), Gas Mark 7, for about 30 minutes. Remove from the oven, sprinkle generously with the vanilla sugar and cut into portions when cool enough to handle.

162

Hungarian Cheesecake

Serves 6–8

Cheesecake was originally baked as old English recipes and those from central Europe indicate. This recipe is from Hungary and includes rum and raisins and is certainly scrumptious. I usually make it the day before serving to allow the flavour and texture to settle. I have also included a typical American set cheesecake to enable a comparison.

Pastry:
4 oz (115 g) plain white flour
2 oz (115 g) plain wholemeal flour
1 oz (30 g) demerara sugar
3 oz (85 g) butter
3 tablespoons cold water

Filling:
1 lb (450 g) curd cheese
$\frac{1}{4}$ pint (150 ml) double cream
4 oz (115 g) caster sugar
3 egg yolks
$\frac{1}{2}$ teaspoon vanilla essence
1$\frac{1}{2}$ oz (45 g) cornflour
2 oz (55 g) candied peel, chopped
4 oz (115 g) seedless raisins
2–3 tablespoons rum
3 egg whites

Make the pastry by mixing the flours and sugar. Rub in the butter until the mixture resembles breadcrumbs. Mix to a dough with the cold water and rest for 10 minutes. Line the base of a greased 8 in (20 cm) springform or loose-bottomed cake tin with buttered paper. Roll out the pastry to fit the base, prick well with a fork and bake in the centre of a moderately hot oven, 400°F (200°C), Gas Mark 6, for 20 minutes. Remove from the oven and turn it down to 300°F (150°C), Gas Mark 2. Make the filling by first sieving the curd cheese if it is lumpy. Mix in the

163

cream, sugar, egg yolks, vanilla, cornflour, peel, raisins and rum, until well combined. Whisk the egg whites until fairly stiff and fold into the cheese mixture. Pour the filling on to the pastry base and bake below the centre of a cool oven for 70 minutes. I then turn the oven off and allow the cheesecake to cool in the oven, because cooked cheesecakes rise during cooking and fall during cooling. After removing the cake from the oven, loosen the clip on the side of the tin and slide the cake, still on its paper, on to a platter for serving at home. Leave in its tin if the cheesecake is to travel.

Strawberry-topped Cheesecake   *Serves 6–8*

This is a gelatine set cheesecake which must be kept very cold in an insulated container while travelling. The strawberries, or any fresh fruit, are added just before serving and it's a good way of making the most of just a few strawberries.

Crumb base:
4 oz (115 g) digestive or wheatmeal biscuits
1 teaspoon ground cinnamon
2 oz (55 g) unsalted butter, melted

Cheesecake:
4 tablespoons water
½ oz (15 g) powdered gelatine
juice and finely grated rind of 1 orange
3 egg yolks
2 oz (55 g) caster sugar
1 lb (450 g) curd cheese
3 egg whites
1 oz (30 g) caster sugar
¼ pint (150 ml) double cream, whipped
strawberries or other fresh fruit

Butter an 8 in (20 cm) loose-bottomed or springform cake tin. Crush the biscuits and cinnamon in a plastic bag with a rolling pin (or stand on them), shake to mix. Pour into a bowl and mix in the melted butter. Turn into the cake tin and press to fit over the base of the tin. Put into the fridge or freezer to harden while you make the filling. Measure the water into a small saucepan, sprinkle on the gelatine and after it has swollen dissolve over gentle heat. Remove from heat as soon as the liquid is clear, pour the orange juice and rind into it and leave in a warm place. Beat the egg yolks and sugar until foamy, then beat in the gelatine mixture in a long thin stream. Beat in the cheese in 2 or 3 additions. In another bowl whisk the egg whites until stiff and fold in the sugar. Now whisk the cream until stiff but still glossy (use the same whisk as for the egg whites, don't wash it). Fold the cream and then the egg whites into the cheese mixture and pour on to the crumb base. Allow to set in a refrigerator for 4 hours at least. Decorate with sugared strawberries or other fresh fruit before serving.

Butterscotch Creams   *Serves 4*

A well setting pudding with a delicate flavour.

4 oz (115 g) dark soft brown sugar
½ pint (275 ml) creamy milk
2 egg yolks
2 oz (55 g) unsalted butter
½ oz (15 g) powdered gelatine
4 tablespoons cold water
2 egg whites, stiffly beaten
whipped cream (optional)
walnuts, chopped (optional)

Cook the sugar, milk and egg yolks together in the top of a double boiler until the mixture just coats the back of a spoon. Remove from heat and strain into a bowl. Add the butter cut in pieces and stir until melted. Soften the gelatine in the cold water and heat gently until dissolved. Pour in a thin stream into the butterscotch mixture, stirring all the time. Set aside to cool and when almost set pour on to the stiffly beaten egg whites and fold in carefully. Spoon into small pots or ramekins. When set the butterscotch creams can be topped with a rosette of whipped cream and some chopped walnuts, if desired.

Quick Orange Jellies

Makes 6

I always keep plenty of frozen fruit juice in the freezer and it makes very good jellies. Small children invariably like jelly (as did Earl Attlee) and I make them in individual pots.

5 teaspoons powdered gelatine
1 pint (425 ml) cold water
6¼ oz (184 g) container concentrated orange juice
a little honey or sugar if desired
crushed meringues or brandy snaps (optional)

Soften the gelatine in 4 tablespoons of the water in a small saucepan. Gently heat until dissolved. Mix the rest of the water with the orange juice and stir well. Add the slightly cooled gelatine in a long thin trickle, stirring all the time. Add honey or sugar to taste, if needed. Pour into small cream pots or cups and allow to set in the fridge. If you wish, sprinkle some crushed meringues or brandy snaps on to the jellies. I prefer not to freeze jellies because the texture deteriorates and they become granular.

Stuffed Peaches

Serves 8

I love this Italian pudding of stuffed peaches. Make it when peaches are really cheap during August.

8 large yellow Italian peaches
2 oz (55 g) ground almonds ⎫
2 oz (55 g) sponge cake crumbs ⎬ or use 4 oz (155 g) marzipan
grated rind and juice of an orange or lemon
2 glasses Italian white wine
1 tablespoon caster sugar

Scald the peaches in boiling water for 1–2 minutes. Lift out and peel away the skins, halve and stone them. Mix the ground almonds, cake crumbs, orange rind and juice together (or work the rind and juice into the marzipan). Divide the mixture between the peaches, sandwiching it between two halves. Place the peaches in a fireproof dish and pour the wine over them. Bake in a moderate oven, 350°F (180°C), Gas Mark 4, for 15 minutes if the peaches are really ripe, otherwise until the peaches are just cooked. Remove from the oven and sprinkle caster sugar over each peach and caramelise under a hot grill. Serve with cream if you wish; I prefer them without, either hot or cold. For travelling I place each peach in a cocotte dish or use an oyster plate.

Small Raspberry Mousses $\qquad$ *Serves 4–6*

Fresh and summery even in the depths of winter. I use small ones in packed lunches or take a large one to a Pot Luck Supper because everyone likes it.

8 oz (225 g) fresh or frozen raspberries
1½ oz (45 g) sugar
2 tablespoons water
2 teaspoons gelatine
¼ pint (150 ml) double cream
2 egg whites
1 tablespoon caster sugar

Cook the raspberries with the sugar and water over moderate heat for only 4–5 minutes to draw the juice. Set aside to cool. In a small saucepan over low heat soften and then dissolve the gelatine in a little of the raspberry juice. Sieve or liquidise the raspberries with their juice and then mix with the dissolved gelatine. Whip the cream until stiff but still glossy and fold into the raspberry purée. Whisk the egg whites until stiff and whisk in the caster sugar, then fold into the mousse. Spoon into individual pots or dishes or one pretty bowl and set in a fridge for 2 hours. For travelling the mousses can, if necessary, be frozen first.

Rich Chocolate Mousses   *Makes 4–6*

What a lovely surprise is a chocolate mousse at the bottom of a briefcase that doubles as a lunch box.

6 oz (170 g) plain chocolate, e.g. Bournville
3 egg yolks
1 teaspoon liquid coffee essence
3 egg whites
1 oz (30 g) vanilla sugar
sprinkling of toasted almonds or chopped walnuts

Break the chocolate into pieces and melt it in a heatproof bowl over a little simmering water. When it is melted, beat in the egg yolks one at a time with the coffee essence. Whisk the egg whites until stiff and fold in the sugar. Gently fold the egg whites into the chocolate mixture in 2 or 3 amounts. Spoon into ramekins or small pots and sprinkle with nuts. Set aside in a cool place for at least an hour. If you wish, replace the coffee with brandy or Cointreau for someone's birthday.

168

Frozen Coffee Mousse (a soft ice cream)

Serves 8

This is a very quick and easy method for making a smooth ice cream which travels well if kept in a well-insulated container.

4 egg whites
4 oz (115 g) caster sugar
4 egg yolks
½ pint (275 ml) double cream
2–3 tablespoons liquid coffee essence
2–3 tablespoons brandy (optional)

Make sure the eggs are at room temperature and then whisk the whites until stiff. Gradually whisk in the sugar in 3 or 4 amounts. Beat the yolks together in a cup and gradually whisk into the whites in spoonfuls. In another bowl beat the cream with the coffee essence until stiff but still glossy. Fold the cream into the eggs with a metal spoon and when well combined spoon into a lidded plastic box. 2–3 tablespoons brandy mixed in with the cream goes down well too. Freeze for 5–6 hours.

Strawberry Ice Cream

Serves 8

Homemade ice cream makes an excellent pudding for a portable meal or picnic if you have an insulated container and an ice pack. Otherwise use a wide-necked vacuum flask — either spoon the ice cream straight into the flask or pack small containers of the ice cream into it. This strawberry ice cream can be made at any time of the year because the strawberries are quickly cooked first to extract the full flavour, so in the winter I use strawberries from the freezer.

1 lb (450 g) strawberries
6 oz (170 g) granulated sugar
12 tablespoons water
3 egg yolks
¾ pint (425 ml) double cream, whipped

Bring the strawberries, 2 oz (55 g) sugar and 4 tablespoons water to the boil in a saucepan. Simmer for 2 minutes then cool and liquidise or sieve. In a small heavy-based saucepan dissolve the rest of the sugar with the rest of the water and boil to the short thread stage or 220°F (105°C), if you have a sugar thermometer. Beat the egg yolks together in a bowl and then pour the slightly cooled sugar syrup in a long thin stream on to the egg yolks, beating steadily until the mixture becomes thick and fluffy. Fold in the cooled strawberry purée and finally fold in the whipped cream. Pour into a lidded plastic container to freeze. This ice cream will not need to be beaten again and will be gorgeously smooth and creamy.

Home-made Yoghurt

One of the cheapest and most nutritious puddings is yoghurt, but not the commercially made curd which is usually too sweet and not cheap. Yoghurt is easy and economical to make at home.

Quite the easiest method is to use U.H.T. long-life milk because this only needs heating to just above blood heat, 120°F or 45°C (marked YOGHURT on a cooking thermometer). If you wish to use fresh milk it is necessary to bring the milk to boiling point, maintain it for at least 1 minute, and then let it cool to yoghurt temperature. When the milk is at the desired temperature simply stir in 1 tablespoon natural yoghurt until there are no lumps. Pour into a warm lidded container (plastic, china or glass — a bowl with a plate on top is fine) or into a pre-warmed vacuum flask. Leave in a warm place, like an airing cupboard or at the back of a boiler or solid fuel stove, on a piece of wood if the surface is hot, for at least 6 hours. I find it best left overnight. Then remove to a cool place and later store in the fridge. The yoghurt will be set and firm and can be spooned out easily to be flavoured or eaten just as it is, with a little honey or ground cinammon. For variety, I have worked out some other ideas for flavouring yoghurt.

Yoghurt Toppings

Home-made yoghurt is very successful with honey, jam or black treacle (children love trailing a spoonful poised high over the yoghurt to make intricate patterns with the finest of lines). Fresh or stewed fruit such as blackberries, mashed banana with raisins, sliced pears or peaches, apple with cinammon are all delicious. Crumbled meringues, brandy snaps or grated chocolate are popular. I also find all the hot sauces that I make for ice cream — chocolate, coffee, fudge, melba, butterscotch — work well added cool to yoghurt. Here are some other ideas.

CRUNCHY NUT TOPPING
2 oz (55 g) rolled oats
1 oz (30 g) desiccated coconut
1 oz (30 g) chopped walnuts
1 oz (30 g) demerara sugar
$\frac{1}{4}$ teaspoon ground cinnamon

Toast the rolled oats and coconut under a hot grill until golden. Tip into a bowl and stir in the walnuts, sugar and cinnamon. Store in a lidded jar.

SULTANAS IN SHERRY

1 oz (30 g) unsalted butter
1 oz (30 g) soft dark brown sugar
3–4 oz (85–115 g) sultanas
1–2 tablespoons sherry

Melt the butter with the sugar in a small saucepan and cook, stirring, for 1 minute. Stir in the sultanas and sherry and cook together, bubbling, for 1 minute. Spoon into a dish and serve hot or cold with chilled yoghurt.

Cakes, Biscuits and Cookies

This chapter is about how to avoid having to buy sweets or snack foods ever again. Some of the recipes are for food that you can end a meal with or food that is nice to pop into a packed meal box as a treat or a corner-filler. I have included some wholemeal recipes because wholemeal flour is very satisfying and it makes cakes and biscuits that are robust enough to travel. Everything in this chapter will freeze for 3–6 months.

All-Bran Fruit Loaf

This is my version of the All-Bran loaf that everyone — from toddlers to grannies — likes. Very easy to make, it is delicious topped with thinly-sliced Edam cheese and apple. This loaf is also very good toasted.

4 oz (115 g) All-Bran cereal
2 tablespoons honey
6 oz dried fruit — raisins, sultanas, currants, dates (whatever you have
    to hand)
½ pint (275 g) hot tea
½ beaten egg or 1 egg yolk
6 oz (170 g) granary or wholemeal flour
2 teaspoons baking powder
½ teaspoon mixed spice

Put the All-Bran, honey and dried fruit in a mixing bowl and pour over the hot tea, mix and leave until cold. Stir in all the rest of the ingredients, mix well and turn into a well greased 1 lb (½ kg) or 1½ pint loaf tin. Bake in the centre of a moderate oven, 350°F (180°C), Gas Mark 4, for 50–60 minutes. Leave in the tin for 5 minutes, then cool on a wire rack.

Wholemeal Fruit Cake

This is a dark fruit cake with a caramel flavour and it is very sustaining.

8 oz (225 g) butter or soft margarine
6 oz (170 g) dark soft brown sugar
2 tablespoons black treacle
3 eggs, beaten
2 teaspoons mixed spice

4 oz (115 g) white self-raising flour, sieved
6 oz (170 g) wholemeal flour
12 oz (340 g) mixed dried fruit — raisins, sultanas, currants
2 oz (55 g) glacé cherries, quartered

Cream the butter or margarine with the brown sugar and treacle until pale and fluffy. Gradually add the beaten eggs. Fold in the sieved white flour and spice and the unsieved wholemeal flour alternately with the dried fruit and cherries. Spoon into two greased 1 lb ($\frac{1}{2}$ kg) or one 2 lb (kg) loaf tins and bake in the centre of a moderate oven, 350°F (180°C), Gas Mark 4, for 1–1$\frac{1}{2}$ hours. Leave to cool in the tin for 10 minutes then turn out and cool on a wire rack.

Wholemeal Chocolate Walnut Cake

A good easy cake for children to make — it's excellent for bicycling picnics.

8 oz (225 g) self-raising wholemeal flour
pinch of salt
$\frac{1}{2}$ teaspoon cinnamon
2$\frac{1}{2}$ oz (70 g) chopped walnuts
4 oz (115 g) butter or margarine
1 oz (30 g) cocoa
1 tablespoon honey
4 oz (115 g) dark soft brown sugar
2 eggs
2 tablespoons milk

Frosting (optional):
1 oz (30 g) butter
2 oz (55 g) dark soft brown sugar
2 teaspoons cocoa
1 tablespoon milk
$\frac{1}{4}$ teaspoon cinnamon

176

Tip the flour, salt, cinnamon and chopped nuts into a mixing bowl. Melt the butter or margarine in a saucepan. Remove from the heat and stir in the cocoa, honey, sugar, eggs and milk. Pour on to the flour mixture and mix well. Turn into a greased 7 in (18 cm) round cake tin or an 8 in (20 cm) square tin. Smooth the mixture level and bake in the centre of a moderate oven, 350°F (180°C), Gas Mark 4, for 45 minutes. Cool in the tin for 3 minutes then turn out to cool on a wire rack.

To make the frosting, melt the butter with the sugar, cocoa, milk and cinnamon. Stir over gentle heat to dissolve the sugar, then raise the heat and allow the frosting to bubble fast for 1 minute. Remove from heat and beat until cool and thickening. Pour over the cake and leave plain or decorate with walnuts.

This cake is also excellent un-iced but sprinkled with sugar.

Jordan's Marmalade Cake

I find Jordan's self-raising wholemeal flour very good. Their recipe for this marmalade cake gives a moist, flavoursome cake which keeps well.

10 oz (290 g) Jordan's Country Cookbook self-raising flour
5 oz (140 g) demerara sugar
1 teaspoon mixed spice
pinch salt
5 oz (140 g) butter or soft margarine
grated rind of 2 oranges
2 tablespoons milk
3 well-rounded tablespoons firm orange marmalade
2 eggs

In a mixing bowl stir the flour, sugar, spice and salt together. Use a knife to cut the butter or margarine into the mixture, using fingertips to rub in if necessary. Mix the orange rind, milk and marmalade together and beat in the eggs. Pour over the dry ingredients and mix together well. Pour the mixture into a greased 7 in (18 cm) round cake tin and bake in the centre of a moderate oven, 350°F (180°C), Gas Mark 4, for 50–60 minutes. Leave to cool in the tin for 5 minutes, then cool on a wire tray. Keep for at least a day before cutting.

Carrot and Orange Cake

This moist cake has a most tantalising flavour — see if anyone can guess the ingredients!

4 oz (115 g) butter or soft margarine
4 oz (115 g) dark soft brown sugar
grated rind of ½ large orange
2 eggs
2 oz (55 g) white self-raising flour, sieved
1 teaspoon baking powder
1 teaspoon ground cinnamon
4 oz (115 g) grated carrot
4 oz (115 g) wholemeal flour

Icing:
1 oz (30 g) butter, softened
1 tablespoon honey
finely grated rind of ½ orange

Cream the butter with the sugar and orange rind until pale and fluffy. Gradually beat in the eggs and then fold in the sieved white flour, baking powder and cinnamon. Stir in half the grated carrot, the wholemeal flour and then the rest of the carrot. Turn into a greased 6½ in (17 cm) round cake tin and bake in a moderate oven, 350°F (180°C), Gas Mark 4, for 1 hour. Leave to cool in the tin for 5 minutes then cool on a wire rack.

While the cake is still warm make the icing. Mix the softened butter with the honey in a cup or small bowl. Spread over the cake and sprinkle with the finely grated rind of the orange.

Chocolate Banana Cake

The bananas give the chocolate cake a delicious moistness, and the cream cheese frosting is a good flavour contrast.

6 oz (170 g) butter or soft margarine
6 oz (170 g) dark soft brown sugar
2 ripe bananas, mashed
3 eggs
7 oz (200 g) self-raising flour
1 oz (30 g) cocoa

Frosting:
3 oz (85 g) cream cheese
6 oz (160 g) icing sugar
1 tablespoon creamy milk
2–3 drops vanilla essence

Cream the butter or margarine with the sugar until fluffy and light. Beat in the mashed bananas and then gradually add the beaten eggs, mixing well. Fold in the sieved flour and cocoa. Turn the mixture into a greased and base-lined 9 in (23 cm) square cake tin and level the top. Bake in the centre of a moderate oven, 350°F (180°C), Gas Mark 4, for 45 minutes. Leave in the tin for 2 minutes and then turn out to cool on a wire rack.

To make the frosting, cream the cream cheese, icing sugar and milk until smooth. Flavour to taste with a few drops of vanilla essence. Spread over the cake and mark into squares when set.

Dorset Apple Cake

I've tried many apple cake recipes over the years and I find this one from Dorset is always popular.

8 oz (225 g) self-raising flour
1 teaspoon ground cinnamon
4 oz (115 g) light soft brown sugar
4 oz (115 g) butter
10 oz (290 g) grated apple, without cores and peel
4 oz (115 g) sultanas
2 oz (55 g) chopped mixed candied peel
2 eggs
2 tablespoons light soft brown sugar

Sieve the flour and cinnamon into a mixing bowl and stir in the sugar. Cut the butter into the mixture with a knife — use finger-tips if necessary to break up the butter. Add the grated apple, sultanas and candied peel. Mix to a soft dough with the beaten eggs. Spread the mixture in a greased 8 in (20 cm) round loose-bottomed tin and sprinkle the surface with the rest of the brown sugar. Bake above the centre of a moderately hot oven 400°F (200°C), Gas Mark 6, for 45 minutes. Allow to cool in the tin then cut into portions.

Lunch Box Cake   *Makes 12 square*

A quick-to-make fruit cake that is cut into squares as soon as it cool.

4 oz (115 g) butter or soft margarine
4 oz (115 g) caster sugar
2 eggs
$\frac{1}{4}$ teaspoon almond essence
5 oz (140 g) self-raising flour
5 oz (140 g) mixed raisins, sultanas and currants

2 oz (55 g) glacé cherries, quartered
1 oz (30 g) chopped candied peel
1 tablespoon granulated sugar

Cream the butter or margarine with the sugar until pale and fluffy. Gradually fold in the sieved flour and also the fruit, cherries and peel until all are well combined. Spoon the mixture into a well greased tin, 10 × 6 in (25 × 15 cm) and 1 in (2.5 cm) deep. Level the top of the mixture with the back of a spoon and sprinkle granulated sugar over the surface. Bake in the centre of a moderate oven, 325°F (170°C), Gas Mark 3, for 50–60 minutes. Leave to cool in the tin and then cut the cake into 12 squares.

Apricot Squares   *Makes 8–12 squares*

Children always enjoy an apricot square and a glass of milk as a mid-morning break.

Apricot filling:
4 oz (115 g) dried apricots
½ pint (275 ml) hot water
1 tablespoon light soft brown sugar
1 teaspoon cornflour
1 tablespoon cold water

Oat crust:
8 oz (225 g) rolled oats
4 oz (115 g) self-raising flour
4 oz (115 g) light soft brown sugar
4 oz (115 g) butter or soft margarine
4 tablespoons milk
1 tablespoon demerara sugar

Chop the apricots or snip with a pair of scissors into a bowl. Pour the hot water over them and leave to soak for 30 minutes. Then simmer over gentle heat for 10 minutes. Blend together in a cup the sugar, cornflour and cold water. Pour on to the apricots and cook the mixture, stirring all the time, until thickened. Set aside to cool. Mix the oats, flour and sugar together in a bowl and rub in the butter or margarine until the mixture is like breadcrumbs. Add 3 tablespoons of the milk and mix to a dough. Roll out half the dough to fit the base of a greased tin, 11 × 7 in (28 × 18 cm). Spread the apricot filling over the base and cover with the rest of the crust rolled out to fit. Brush with the rest of the milk and sprinkle with demerara sugar. Prick all over with a fork. Bake above the centre of a moderate oven, 350°F (180°C), Gas Mark 4, for 35 minutes. Allow to cool in the tin, but mark in squares straight away using a sharp knife. Remove from the tin when completely cool.

Chocolate Pineapple Squares   Makes 24–30

I find a small square of this cross between a biscuit and a cake replaces bought sweets admirably.

7 oz (200 g) plain chocolate
2 oz (55 g) butter
4 oz (115 g) light soft brown sugar
2 oz (55 g) plain flour
2 oz (55 g) desiccated coconut
4 oz (115 g) pineapple, drained and crushed
2–3 oz (55–85 g) glacé cherries, chopped

Well grease a swiss roll tin, 13 × 9 in (32 × 23 cm). Melt the chocolate in a small bowl over hot water and pour into the tin. Spread evenly and leave to set or pop the tin into the fridge or freezer. Melt the butter and add the sugar, sieved flour, coconut pineapple and cherries. Mix well and then spread the mixture over the set chocolate. Bake in a moderately hot oven, 400°F (200°C), Gas Mark 6, for 15–20 minutes until the mixture is golden. Cool in the tin, then allow to get very cold in the fridge or freezer. Turn upside down over a wooden board or work surface. Put a very hot damp cloth over the base of the tin to soften the chocolate just enough for the whole biscuit to unmould from the tin. Remove the tin, allow the chocolate to re-harden for a few minutes, then turn over and cut into 24–30 squares.

Grasmere Gingerbread   *Makes 16 fingers*

This crumbly shortbread is from the Lake District.

4 oz (115 g) plain flour
4 oz (115 g) light soft brown sugar
$\frac{1}{4}$ teaspoon baking powder
1 teaspoon ground ginger
4 oz (115 g) fine or medium oatmeal
finely grated rind of $\frac{1}{2}$ lemon
finely grated rind of $\frac{1}{2}$ orange
4 oz (115 g) slightly salted butter

Sieve the flour, sugar, baking powder and ground ginger into a mixing bowl. Add the oatmeal and the finely grated rinds and stir together. Melt the butter and add to the mixture. Use a knife to work the butter in but leave the mixture still crumbly. Lightly press into a well-buttered 10 × 6 in (25 × 15 cm) tin. Bake in the centre of a slow oven, 325°F (160°C), Gas Mark 3, for 30 minutes until golden. Remove from the oven and cut into 16 fingers but leave to cool in the tin. This is scrumptious topped with whipped cream and sprinkled with diced preserved ginger.

Healthfood Flapjack

Makes 12–15 squares

I cut this into squares. One piece of this and I can dig over the whole of my leek patch!

6 oz (170 g) butter or margarine
4 oz (115 g) demerara sugar
2 oz (55 g) syrup
4 oz (115 g) sultanas
8 oz (225 g) rolled oats
2 oz (30 g) sesame seeds
2 tablespoons bran
2 tablespoons wheatgerm

In a saucepan melt the butter or margarine with the sugar and syrup. Remove from heat, add the sultanas and stir well. Mix in the oats, seeds, bran and wheatgerm and pour into a well greased tin, 11 × 7 in (28 × 18 cm). Smooth the mixture level and bake above the centre of a moderate oven, 350°F (180°C), Gas Mark 4, for 30–35 minutes until golden brown. Mark into 12 or 15 pieces with a knife and leave until cold before cutting through completely and removing the squares from the tin.

Treacle Girdle Scones

Makes 12

Spread these drop scones with cream cheese instead of butter to accentuate their flavour.

4 oz (115 g) self-raising flour
$\frac{1}{4}$ teaspoon salt
grated nutmeg
2 teaspoons caster sugar
1 oz (30 g) butter
1 egg
1 tablespoon black treacle

184

5 tablespoons milk
2 oz (55 g) seedless raisins or sultanas

Sieve the flour and salt into a bowl, grate nutmeg on to the surface and stir in the sugar. Cut the butter into the flour and when fine enough add the egg beaten with the treacle and the milk. Beat until smooth. Heat a griddle or heavy-based frying pan and grease with a little oil or margarine. Drop tablespoons of the mixture on to the griddle, and when the bubbles begin to rise sprinkle each scone with some raisins. After 2–3 minutes turn the scones over and cook on the other side for about 3 minutes. Keep warm in a cloth and make the other griddle cakes with the rest of the mixture. These scones freeze splendidly and can be reheated under the grill or in a hot oven for a few minutes, or even in a greased frying pan over a camp fire.

Oat and Raisin Cookies   *Makes about 36*

These cookies are so simple to make — mixed in a saucepan, a crisp cookie with a soft centre.

4 oz (115 g) margarine
6 oz (170 g) light soft brown sugar
1 egg, beaten
8 oz (225 g) rolled oats
2 oz (55 g) wholemeal flour
$\frac{1}{2}$ teaspoon bicarbonate of soda
4 oz (115 g) seedless raisins

Melt the margarine in a saucepan, stir in the sugar and then the beaten egg. Tip in the oats, flour, bicarbonate of soda and raisins. Mix until well combined. Take a dessertspoonful, roll into a ball in your hands, and flatten slightly on to a greased baking sheet. Continue until all the mixture is used, then bake in the centre of a moderate oven, 350°F (180°C), Gas Mark 4, for

10–12 minutes until golden. Allow to cool for a few minutes, then lift off the baking sheet with a flat knife and cool the cookies on a wire rack.

Sultana and Marmalade Biscuits   *Makes 30*

These are crisp and buttery biscuits that travel well.

12 oz (340 g) plain flour
1 teaspoon baking powder
5 oz (140 g) demerara sugar
5 oz (140 g) butter
3 oz (85 g) sultanas
2 tablespoons orange marmalade
1 tablespoon hot water
1 egg
a little extra demerara sugar

Sieve the flour and baking powder into a bowl. Stir in the sugar and cut the butter into the mixture until in very small pieces, using fingertips if necessary to rub it in. Stir in the sultanas. Mix the marmalade with the hot water and beat in the egg. Add the liquid to the flour mixture and mix to a soft dough. On a floured board roll out the dough to just under ¼ in (½ cm) thickness, and cut out cookies with a 2½ in (6.5 cm) plain cutter. Sprinkle each cookie with a little demerara sugar. Bake on a greased baking sheet in a moderate oven, 350°F (180°C), Gas Mark 4, for 15–18 minutes until just golden at the edges.

Sesame Seed Biscuits   *Makes 24*

Excellent corner-fillers — also good to nibble with a drink.

6 oz (170 g) plain flour
pinch of onion salt
2 oz (55 g) butter or soft margarine
2 oz (55 g) grated cheese — red Cheshire or Leicester

186

2 tablespoons sesame seeds
1 egg yolk plus 1 tablespoon of milk *or* 2½ tablespoons milk

Sieve the flour and onion salt into a bowl. Cut the butter or margarine into the flour until in very small pieces. Add the grated cheese and 1½ tablespoons of sesame seeds. Mix to a soft dough with the egg yolk and milk. On a floured board roll the dough out to ¼ in (½ cm) thickness. Sprinkle surface with the rest of the seeds and roll the dough just a little thinner. Use a fluted 2 in (5 cm) cutter to cut 24 biscuits. (For biscuits with drinks use a 1 in (2.5 cm) cutter.) Bake on a greased baking sheet in a moderate oven, 375°F (190°C), Gas Mark 5, for 15 minutes. Cool on a wire rack.

Crunchy Bacon Squares

Good for eating with soup or alone as a snack.

4 rashers smoked streaky bacon
1 clove garlic, crushed
small knob of butter
4 oz (115 g) plain white flour
4 oz (115 g) wholemeal or granary flour
2 oz (55 g) butter or margarine
½ teaspoon dried herbs
4–5 tablespoons cold water

Fry the bacon until crisp with the crushed garlic in the knob of butter. Cool on a plate and use scissors to dice the bacon. Sieve the plain flour into a bowl, add the wholemeal flour and cut in the butter or margarine, using fingertips to rub in if necessary. Stir in the bacon, garlic and herbs and mix to a soft dough with 4–5 tablespoons of cold water. On a floured board roll the dough out to just over ¼ in (½ cm) thickness. Cut small squares, strips or circles and bake on a greased baking sheet above the centre of a hot oven, 400°F (200°C), Gas Mark 6, for 10–12 minutes. Cool on a wire rack.

Cheese and Peanut Triangles   *Makes about 36*

These crunchy savoury biscuits are much more wholesome
than packets of crisps and other snack food. I always keep a
selection of savoury biscuits in the freezer to pop into the corner
of a lunch box or to munch on a long car journey.

4 oz (115 g) plain white flour
$\frac{1}{4}$ teaspoon cayenne pepper
$\frac{1}{4}$ teaspoon dried mustard
4 oz (115 g) granary or wholemeal flour
4 oz (115 g) butter or soft margarine
4 oz (115 g) Cheddar cheese, grated
2 oz (55 g) salted peanuts, chopped
1 egg yolk

Sieve the white flour, pepper and mustard into a mixing bowl.
Stir in the granary flour. Cut the butter into the flours and rub in
until the mixture resembles breadcrumbs. Add the cheese and
nuts and bind to a soft dough with the egg yolk plus a little milk if
necessary. On a floured board roll the dough out to $\frac{1}{4}$ in ($\frac{1}{2}$ cm)
thickness. Cut into triangles — the mixture should make about
36 small 2–3 in (5–7 cm) triangles. Place on a greased baking
sheet and bake in a hot oven, 400°F (200°C), Gas Mark 6, for
15–20 minutes until golden and crisp. Cool on a wire rack.

Oatcakes   *Makes 8 farls*

These famous Scottish biscuits go well with cheese and pâté.

8 oz (225 g) medium oatmeal
$\frac{1}{4}$ teaspoon bicarbonate of soda
$\frac{1}{4}$ teaspoon salt
1 tablespoon dripping or lard
6–8 tablespoons hot water

Mix the oatmeal, bicarbonate of soda and salt together. In a small saucepan melt the dripping with the hot water. Pour on to the oatmeal and stir with a wooden spoon until a soft dough is formed. Knead into a ball with your hand and divide in two with a knife. Roll out each half to form a circle $\frac{1}{8}$ in (3 mm) thick. Cut round a 7 in (18 cm) diameter teaplate to make a bannock. Divide into quarters to make farls. Bake on a greased baking sheet in a moderate oven at 350°F (180°C), Gas Mark 4, for 25 minutes. Cool on a wire rack. Store in an airtight container and if possible recrisp in the oven or under the grill before serving.

Digestive Biscuits   *Makes about 18*

Home-made digestive biscuits are rather a treat — good with cheese or dipped in melted chocolate!

4 oz (115 g) 100% wholemeal flour
4 oz (115 g) medium oatmeal
1 oz (30 g) light brown sugar
$\frac{1}{4}$ teaspoon bicarbonate of soda
3 oz (85 g) salted butter
1 egg yolk

Mix the flour, oatmeal, sugar and bicarbonate of soda together in a bowl. Cut the butter into the mixture and rub in as for pastry. Mix to a dough with the egg yolk. Roll out on a floured board to $\frac{1}{8}$ in (3 mm) thickness. Cut rounds with a $2\frac{1}{2}$ in (6.5 cm) plain cutter. Bake on a greased baking sheet in the centre of a moderate oven, 350°F (180°C), Gas Mark 4, for 15 minutes. Leave to cool on a baking sheet for 3 minutes then cool on a wire tray.

Wholewheat Cheese Shortbread   *Makes 24*

An excellent accompaniment to a creamy vegetable soup.

6 oz (170 g) butter or soft margarine
1 clove garlic
$\frac{1}{4}$ teaspoon salt
good pinch cayenne pepper
freshly milled black pepper
8 oz (225 g) grated cheese — strong Cheddar is good
8 oz (225 g) plain wholemeal flour

Soften the butter or margarine in a bowl. Crush the garlic with the salt and beat into the butter with the peppers. Work the grated cheese and the flour into the butter until all are combined into a soft dough. On a floured board roll out the dough to $\frac{1}{4}$ in ($\frac{1}{2}$ cm) thickness. Cut plain rounds with a $2\frac{1}{2}$ in (6.5 cm) cutter. Prick with a fork and bake on a greased baking sheet in a moderate oven, 375°F (190°C), Gas Mark 5, for 12–15 minutes. Cool on a wire rack.

Variation: add 2 teaspoons curry paste to the butter and then add the rest of the ingredients and proceed as above. I make a criss-cross design on these biscuits to show that they are curry flavoured.

Drinks

I much prefer to accompany a meal with a drink, ideally a glass of wine, but otherwise cool fresh water. Since often neither of these is possible or desirable when eating a packed meal I have gathered together some alternative suggestions which I have found very popular with toddlers to grannies. It's worth acquiring a reliable container for drinks, preferably an insulated flask that will keep liquids hot or cold. Most of these drinks are very quick to prepare. Although it usually makes things easier if you plan ahead, many of these recipes simply depend upon a well-stocked store cupboard or freezer.

Fruit-based Drinks

I try to avoid using commercially made fruit squashes and fizzy drinks; they are high in unnecessary sugar and other additives such as artificial colouring, and often leave you even thirstier.

Fresh fruit juice or frozen, bottled or canned juices work much better as drinks especially if served with a little imagination, for example adding some Zesty Ice-cubes (see recipe below) or by mixing an unusual combination.

QUICK ORANGE (OR GRAPEFRUIT) SQUASH
6 oz (170 g) container frozen concentrated orange juice
1 container warm water
2 tablespoons honey

Pour the concentrated orange juice into a jug. Fill the container with warm water and stir the honey into it. Mix the liquid with the juice and stir well. Pour into a screw-topped bottle and store in a fridge for up to 2 weeks. Dilute with at least the same amount of water before drinking, then add some Zesty Ice-cubes.

ZESTY ICE-CUBES
1 tablespoon clear honey
2 tablespoons very finely chopped mint
1 tablespoon grated rind of an orange or lemon
1 pint (570 ml) cold water
1 orange or lemon

Mix the honey with the chopped mint and the orange or lemon rind. This will extract the aromatic oils from the herb and the rind. Then stir in the water. Store in the freezer or freezing compartment of the fridge until turning to slush. Wash the orange or lemon and cut into very thin slices, cut the slices into pieces that will fit into the ice-cube divisions and put one or two in each. Stir the minted slush and pour into the ice-cube tray

GHTF-7

and freeze for 3–4 hours until solid. When making ice-cubes for a party, I decant the cubes into a lidded plastic container and keep them in the freezer while making extra batches.

LIQUIDISER LEMONADE

Before I owned a liquidiser I was always amazed at how quickly friends used to make this very good drink. I can remember feeling very surprised to see that the whole lemon disappeared into the drink.

1 lemon, thin skinned if possible
1 tablespoon honey, glucose or sugar
2 tablespoons ice-cubes
1 pint (570 ml) cold water

Wash the lemon and cut into quarters. Put all the ingredients into the liquidiser, cover and whizz on maximum speed for 5 seconds or until the lemon has been reduced to a pulp. Strain (or drink complete!) into a jug and serve with more ice-cubes. Perfect after tennis or cricket on a hot afternoon.

TOMATO JUICE

A marvellous all-year-round standby, excellent for slimmers. Makes $\frac{3}{4}$ pint (425 ml) juice very cheaply.

14 oz (400 g) tin peeled tomatoes
1 teaspoon clear honey
$\frac{1}{2}$ teaspoon salt
dash of Worcester sauce
2 tablespoons cold water

Simply tip all the ingredients except the water into a liquidiser, cover and whizz on maximum speed for 5 seconds. Turn into a sieve over a jug or a bowl. Swish round the liquidiser with the cold water and tip into the sieve and stir the juice through the sieve. Chill before serving, if wished.

CARIBBEAN COOLER
14 oz (400 g) tin guavas
1 pint (570 ml) pineapple juice
ice-cubes
small glass of curaçao (optional)

Tip the guavas into a liquidiser and whizz to a purée. Strain
through a sieve into a jug. Stir in the pineapple juice and serve
with ice-cubes plus a little curaçao if you wish.

FRESH APPLE DRINK
3 medium eating apples with good flavour
juice and rind of $\frac{1}{2}$ lemon
1 pint (570 ml) boiling water

Wash the apples and cut into thin slices across. Put them in a jug
or bowl and sprinkle with the lemon juice and a strip of the rind.
Pour on the boiling water, cover and allow to cool for some
hours. Then strain off the apple drink, only sweeten if necessary, and chill before serving.

PINEPRICOT JUICE
1 lb (450 g) freshly poached or tinned apricots, stoned and in their
    syrup
1 pint (570 ml) pineapple juice
mint, finely chopped
small glass dry vermouth (optional)

Tip the stoned apricots into a liquidiser and reduce to a purée.
Add the pineapple juice and whizz to mix. Pour into a glass jug,
sprinkle with finely chopped mint and serve with ice-cubes. Add
some dry Italian vermouth if you need a pick-me-up.

Milk-based Drinks

Fresh milk must be kept very cold to retain all its food value and to my taste to keep it appetising. Make sure that your vacuum flask is pre-cooled with ice-cubes or iced water before pouring in refigerator-cooled milk.

If you find standard fresh milk has no appeal for you or your family it might be worth trying homogenised milk sold in tall glass bottles with a shelf life of several weeks, or the U.H.T. long-life milk with a shelf life of several months (this milk is excellent for taking on holiday when milk supplies may be uncertain). My children prefer both these milks — they have a creamy slightly caramel taste caused by the heat-treated natural sugars in the milk. These longer-life milks make good drinks because they don't separate as easily as fresh milk. I wouldn't recommend evaporated or condensed milk for drinking; one tastes canned and the other is ridiculously sweet. Skimmed dried milk could be used but only if you are dieting; long-life skimmed milk tastes better and has no additives.

CHOCOLATE MILK
This is such a popular drink it is sold in dairies and supermarkets here and on the Continent, which always amazes me when it is so easy to make.

1 tablespoon drinking chocolate powder
1 tablespoon hot water
$\frac{1}{2}$ pint (275 ml) cold milk

In a jug mix the drinking chocolate with the hot water to make a paste. Gradually pour in the milk, stirring all the time. Chill in the fridge before serving.

FRUIT-FLAVOURED MILK

It is difficult to flavour milk with fresh fruit, due to the action of the fruit acid which makes the milk separate. But fruits with low acid content, like bananas, will work well.

BANANA MILK

1 large ripe banana
2 teaspoons honey or sugar
½ pint (275 ml) cold milk

Mash the banana well with the honey or sugar and gradually add the milk, stirring all the time. Strain or pour into a container, or put all the ingredients in a liquidiser and give it a 10-second whizz. Chill before serving. To make banana milk even more sustaining, you can add a beaten egg which will give the drink a splendid head of froth when made in the liquidiser.

BLACKCURRANT MILK

½ pint (275 ml) cold milk
1 tablespoon blackcurrant syrup

Simply pour the milk into a jug or container and gradually add the blackcurrant syrup, stirring all the time. The only thing to remember is to always add the syrup to the milk and not the other way round, because it is easy to curdle the milk. You can use other fruit syrups and commercially-made powders but they do taste rather artificial. Warm, strained, strongly-flavoured jam or jelly can give quite a pleasant drink when added to cold milk.

CARAMEL MILK

½–1 tablespoon black treacle or molasses
½ pint (275 ml) cold or hot milk

Heat the spoon before measuring the treacle and then whisk into the cold or hot milk. Chill if serving cold.

Fruit Punch

This is a splendid thirst-quencher on a long journey.

1 pint (570 ml) cold strained tea (China or weak Indian)
1–2 tablespoons clear honey
¾ pint (425 ml) orange juice
¾ pint (425 ml) pineapple juice
1 large bottle ginger ale
1 orange ⎤
1 apple ⎦ or whatever other fresh fruit is available
6 Zesty Ice-cubes (see p. 193)

Sweeten the tea with honey. Add the fruit juices and store in the fridge with the bottle of ginger ale until really chilled. Cut the fruit into slices. Pour the punch into a large insulated container, add the fruit and the ice-cubes. Pack the bottle of ginger ale in a damp cloth or newspaper for travelling. Pour into the punch just before serving so that the punch doesn't lose its fizz.

This punch is also good with white wine replacing the cold tea.

Lemon Barley Water

Recommended for the kidneys! Very refreshing on a hot summer's day — you don't have to have played tennis first.

2 oz (55 g) pearl barley
rind and juice of a lemon
2 pints (1¼ litres) cold water
honey to sweeten, if desired

Put the pearl barley in a coffee grinder or a powerful liquidiser and whizz on maximum speed for 1 minute. Turn the barley into a saucepan with the thinly pared rind of the lemon and the cold water. Bring to the boil and simmer gently for 10 minutes, stirring from time to time. Strain through a finely meshed sieve into a jug. Add honey to taste and the juice of the lemon. Set aside to cool. Serve chilled with ice-cubes or hot in cold weather.

Grape Juice Cocktail

1 large bottle grape juice
1 large bottle ginger ale
ice-cubes
½ lemon

Refrigerate the bottles as long as possible and then pack them wrapped in a damp cloth near the ice-cubes in an insulated container. Just before serving, pour the grape juice and ginger ale into a jug and add the ice-cubes and lemon cut into slices.

Shopper's Lifeline

This is a meal-replacing drink that is good at any time of the year. I make sure that I leave a flask of this in the car while I'm shopping so that each time I return to the car laden with packages I can build up my energy again.

½ pint (275 ml) milk
1 egg
juice of an orange

Simply blend the milk, egg and orange juice in a liquidiser or whisk together. Pour into a pre-cooled flask, preferably one with its own mug.

June Champagne

My daughter makes this delightful drink as soon as the elder-flower is out. It takes 2–3 weeks to mature and is therefore beautifully timed for midsummer picnics.

3 heads of elderflower in full bloom
rind and juice of 1 lemon or orange
2 tablespoons wine vinegar
1½ lb (680 g) granulated sugar
8 pints (4.5 litres) cold water
6 champagne or sparkling wine bottles plus corks and wires

Cut the large stems from the heads of elderflower and put the blossom into a large bowl or bucket. Add the finely grated rind and juice of the lemon or orange, the vinegar and sugar. Pour in the cold water and stir well. Let the mixture stand for 24 hours, stirring from time to time. Next day strain into bottles and cork and wire them (if you are careful they can be re-used). Store the bottles on their sides in a cool, dark place for 2–3 weeks. The wine is ready when the corks start to rise in the wires. The Colemans of Clyst Hydon, who gave us this recipe, also recommend replacing the lemon with a mugful of black-currants.

Hot Drinks

Many people get a great deal of pleasure from drinking tea or coffee from a vacuum flask — *chacun à son goût* — I much prefer mine freshly made. I find a better alternative is to store plain hot water in a flask and make a hot drink at the time I want it with a tea or coffee bag, yeast extract or blackcurrant syrup. If you have room the best plan is to boil the water freshly on a little spirit or solid fuel burner and it's decidedly more fun. But you may feel that on some occasions, like a day's shooting, a hip flask full of amber liquid is the answer.

GAELIC COFFEE

This is one of the best drinks for cold weather. Friends are delighted when you can produce it from your basket.

Strong black coffee to fill vacuum flask
Scotch or Irish whisky
1 small carton of double cream
sugar if desired
a dessertspoon for pouring

Brew the coffee and pour into a pre-heated vacuum flask. Pack the whisky and cream and sugar securely. To serve pour coffee into each cup, sweeten if desired and add a measure of whisky to each. Then add the cream by pouring it over the back of the dessertspoon into each cup so that the cream rests on the surface of the coffee. Drinking the fortified coffee through the layer of cream is pure heaven.

HOT MARSHMALLOW CHOCOLATE

A popular hot drink to restore you after a winter's hike.

1 pint (570 ml) milk
½ pint (275 ml) water
4–6 tablespoons drinking chocolate powder
1 packet of marshmallows

Heat the milk with the water, or use all milk, if you prefer. Whisk in the chocolate powder when really hot and stir until dissolved. Pour the chocolate into a pre-warmed vacuum flask for traveling. Stir the drink well before serving in mugs, then float 3 or 4 marshmallows on top of each mug of chocolate and watch them melt as you drink.

Getting it all together

Today is a crisp autumn day with bright sunshine. So I shall take my lunch into the garden and plan a family picnic for the weekend. The cider apples are ready to be gathered, to be taken down to the village to the cider press. If it's fine on Saturday we'll invite some friends over to help. I shall carry the hay box full of Jacket Potatoes to the orchard and serve them with Bacon and Sweetcorn Filling and perhaps a Red Cabbage Salad; followed by a huge Apple Pie with Cheese Pastry topped with clotted cream. We should be able to collect about a ton of apples after that!

By serving such food outside, or at least away from the kitchen or dining room, a simple meal can become a movable feast. It is an ideal way to entertain because an infectious air of jollity is part of such an informal occasion and everyone shares any chores.

Every day millions of packed lunches are prepared, but how many are eagerly consumed? I know that a fair amount of bartering goes on among schoolchildren with packed lunches, often because they are bored by their food. Variety is essential in all eating but especially in regular packed food. Try not to pack sandwiches more than once or twice a week, and even then vary the kind and shape of bread — sliced bread one day, rolls another. At least once a week include a salad that is a complete meal and another day pack a hot meal in a wide-necked insulated container. A wedge of home-made pie or some pâté could easily complete the week's menu. I always start to assemble a packed meal by reckoning on the protein-containing (and body building) food and then adding the vitamin-rich food, some roughage and finally a pudding which should complement the other foods.

5-DAY PACKED LUNCH MENU
Chicken Salad with Celery and Pineapple, Granary roll
Raspberry Mousse and 2 Oat and Raisin Cookies

Pumpernickel sandwiches with ham or cheese filling and some
sprigs of watercress
Home-made Yoghurt with Apricots

Hot Boston Pork'n'Beans with Chicory and Orange Salad
A small Apple Pie

Red Bean Salad and 2 Stuffed Eggs
A pear and a piece of Healthfood Flapjack

Wedge of Pork Pie or a Pasty with carrot and celery sticks
A small Orange Jelly and a slice of Treacle Sultana Bread

Drinks can either be milk, fruit juice or hot water to brew up
with, or drinks may be available at school or work. Nuts, dried
and fresh fruit are all excellent corner-fillers rather than bought
sweets or snack foods. Weight-watchers can simply omit the
puddings and have an apple instead. My family take these
packed lunches and whether they are walking, cycling, driving
or using the school bus the food arrives intact and appetising.

Some schools are treating packed lunches sensibly. They make
arrangements for the lunch boxes to be stored in the dining area
at the start of the day until midday, thereby discouraging children from nibbling during the morning. Those schools which
are banning drinks deserve deputations of parents to persuade
them to change their minds. Most children are thirsty at midday
and if drinks from home are banned the schools must provide
water to drink instead. The best schools have taken advantage
of the trend to packed lunches and have built some teaching
about basic nutrition into the curriculum.

Finally I advise trying to plan packed lunches as part of the normal household catering. For example, when I have served a cake or tea-bread if there is any over I slice it and wrap the slices separately before storing them in the freezer. Then it is so simple to add a slice of fruit cake or whatever to a lunch box. Cooked dishes which will reheat well can also be stored in this way.

Food for car journeys must be easy to eat, especially if it is to be eaten while actually travelling. I find the best technique here is to pack each person's food separately. Use plastic boxes or baskets lined with a napkin; a container with sides helps to keep the foods under control. Each person can then eat independently if necessary, which is a boon if you are sharing the driving on a long journey. A siphon vacuum flask is an excellent way of carrying liquids on a journey. Fill the pre-warmed flask with hot water, tea, coffee or chocolate and each person's drink is easily dispensed without spilling or cooling the rest of the drink. Older people who might find a conventional flask difficult to pour can use these flasks with ease.

For car journeys in hot weather avoid sticky sweet food that simply gives everyone a tremendous thirst — if you are drinking a lot you may be stopping a lot, not always easily possible. Salads, individually packed, covered with cling film and kept cold in an insulated box work well on car journeys. Always provide plenty of fresh fruit — the fructose is most restoring. But some drinks are essential, and fortified drinks like Banana Milk or Shopper's Lifeline are excellent. Those travellers inclined to car sickness should stick to carbonated drinks like Grape Juice Cocktail. I try to avoid sandwiches in cars; filled rolls seem much more appetising and pizza, if you can serve it hot, makes a good travelling meal. If you intend to break your journey for an hour or so, and it is advisable to have a break every two hours when driving, then all the picnic possibilities are open to you. We have had splendid meals in meadows or at the motorway picnic spots, especially in France and Germany, where tables, benches and drinking water are usually provided. Then a good meal and a rest, often with a marvellous view, make the whole journey enjoyable.

A few words of advice on food for boat, aeroplane and train travel. It's as well to bear in mind that space is often at a premium, certainly in aeroplanes and Hovercraft. So keep the food compact; sandwiches can come into their own and it's often better to buy some good *café filtré* on a cross-channel ferry than carting around your own drink. Make the food easy to eat and pack it in a disposable container. Wrap food like a pastry or pie in cling film and use a paper cup, plate and napkin carried in a plastic bag, all of which can be dumped in a waste bin afterwards. Steer clear of milk on boats, buses and aeroplanes — for those prone to travel sickness fruit juice is wiser. Make sure to carry some nuts or chocolate to see you through delays at airports and stations.

I particularly enjoy catering for a summer evening, perhaps as a prelude to an evening of outdoor entertainment such as a Greek play or a school Shakespeare or maybe during the long interval at Glyndebourne. This is an opportunity to travel with a meal that is light but appetising and preferably memorable — to match the evening's performance, I hope.

This was a meal that we all remember picnicking with before a Son et Lumière evening in the grounds of a beautiful manor, but it would also be suitable for lunch at the races or at a school sports day.

SUMMER PICNIC
Gazpacho
Terrine of Duck with Orange, Granary Rolls
Salad of Broad Beans
Liptauer Cheese

Stuffed Peaches
Coffee

A dryish white wine or some Beaujolais goes well with this meal. And don't forget the anti-midge cream, or light cigars!

If you find yourself invited to a Pot Luck Supper, where everyone takes a savoury and/or sweet dish it is more fun to take something that looks decorative and that tastes good. These social events are very popular in America and derive from our own Harvest Suppers. All the food is laid out on long trestle tables and everyone serves themselves, sampling as many dishes as possible — although I have seen some very conservative people who insist on eating only the food they brought! A pie always looks festive (and pie-making is one of the dying crafts!) for such occasions, especially if you decorate the lid with pastry leaves and the words Pot Luck Supper. I find a Chicken and Pimento Pie goes down well or a large fruit pie. Also try a Meat Loaf Ring filled with salad or Hungarian Goulash with rice.

From time to time my husband has been a weekly commuter. He stays at his flat during the week and returns home at weekends. He is prepared to reheat food but not to cook it! So I usually pack up a box of complete meals which are simple to reheat in the oven or on top of the stove. The food travels in an insulated box and is stored in the fridge and its freezing compartment as soon as he arrives.

5-DAY PREPARED MEALS MENU
A good mixed salad, arranged ready to eat on a platter with cold ham, tongue or beef. Cover with cling film and keep refrigerated. A salad dressing is packed separately in a screw-top jar.

Canadian Raisin Pie and Cream

A small Shepherd's Pie and Mushrooms à la Grecque
Individual Rich Chocolate Mousse

Bortsch
Beef Curry and Cooked Rice (in a boil-in bag), mango chutney
Hungarian Cheesecake or fresh fruit

Carbonnade Flamande with a Jacket Potato and a vegetable
Butterscotch Cream

Lamb Chops Boulangère followed by Ratatouille (served hot or
cold)
Home-made Yoghurt and Fruit Cake

If I have to be away from home for a few days I make sure I leave
the fridge full of similar meals to those above, plus plenty of eggs
for omelettes and cheese for munching and toasting. I always
leave a good-sized fruit cake or a tea-bread so that no one
complains they went hungry. To save time when preparing food
for reheating, I simply double or treble the size of casseroled
dishes and freeze the surplus in meal-sized packs.

Now that we are moving into the post-industrial age most of us
(willingly or not) are going to have more leisure. We are going to
be able to spend more time at craft and country fairs, point-to-
points and stately homes (the membership of the National Trust
is soaring). Although often absorbing, I find these occasions can
be very tiring, especially if held under canvas. The queues for
food and drinks are often ridiculous and I much prefer to be
self-sufficient. Plenty of drinks are essential, served really cold in
hot weather and piping hot if the weather is inclement. Often it is
easy and more comfortable to return to your vehicle in the car
park where you can indulge in what the Americans call 'a
tail-board picnic' — eating out of the back of the car with your
own picnic stove and food.

ALL-WEATHER PICNIC
Celery and Green Pepper Soup
Game Pie
Tomato or Leek and Bacon Salad
Frozen Coffee Mousse
Grasmere Shortbread

I have two young cousins at school not far away whose parents are working abroad. They reckon the ideal day out is for friends to arrive with transport and a picnic, or, even better, equipment for a barbecue. We have had some very enjoyable days in the Blackdown hills cooking our own lunch. I recommend for a

BARBECUE LUNCH OR SUPPER
Hot Tomato Soup in mugs while watching the kebabs cook
Pork Kebabs or Picnic Parcels
Garlic or Herb bread (heated in foil over the fire)
Strawberry Ice Cream or Chocolate Banana Cake

Even a quite ordinary picnic can be enlivened by taking a fondue set with a spirit burner along, so long as you set it up away from a breeze.

Walkers, climbers, back-packers and sailors usually have to carry their food with them. It's therefore important to keep the weight to a minimum but still provide a meal that is nutritious and tempting. Pasties, filled rolls and sandwiches are often the most practicable, wrapped in cling film or packed in light plastic boxes. Drinks are very important after physical exertion and fruit-based ones are probably preferable to milk ones if the liquid is likely to be shaken around while travelling. I always include a few high-energy foods such as Chocolate Pineapple Squares or Healthfood Flapjacks which can restore those whose spirits are flagging after a cross-country hike, or what-ever.

When off on holiday to a rented cottage or villa miles from the nearest shop I pack plenty of food that will travel well and that will be a welcome addition to our holiday cuisine. This is the kind of food to make ahead and keep in the fridge if you are staying at home but planning a holiday from the kitchen, or you may just be painting it! And if you are caravanning most have a small fridge which will accommodate some Minestrone Soup, a bowl of Rillettes or a Rabbit Terrine, and a well-tempered dish for reheating like Chicken with Paprika and Cummin. And a Wholemeal Fruit Cake and some cookies make good standbys.

Harvest time has always been a traditional time for a movable feast and these occasions have given us some of the best travelling food — huge savoury pies, farmhouse cheeses and large jugs of cider or ale. Often these foods can't be bettered when providing a sustaining lunch or supper after hard work in the fields, vineyards or garden. I remember a specially good harvest lunch while gathering grapes in a German vineyard a few years ago. A dozen of us plus the food were transported to the sloping hillside vineyard in a rough wooden trailer drawn by a tractor. Just as we arrived the wheels ran off the track and the trailer lurched over on its side. We were all thrown on top of each other but there was no damage and it made a very friendly start to a most congenial day! The harvest picnic survived admirably and we were served with a sumptuous selection of pâtés, smoked sausages, cheeses, rye breads and lots of white wine. So if your transport arrangements are uncertain I recommend such a menu.

TRAVELLING FOOD EQUIPMENT
Now that you've prepared your travelling food and drink it is important that it stays in first-rate condition until served and eaten. And this is where acquiring or improvising some equipment specially for the job is well worthwhile.

Most travelling food falls naturally into two groups, cold food and hot food. Too often food from both groups ends up at the end of the journey at the same temperature — an unappetising lukewarm. Not only is this unpalatable but it may also be a health hazard, so the question of food temperature and its maintenance is important.

In the past damp cloths and newspapers plus a block of ice were used to keep food cool. Today life is much easier if you have an *insulated box*, made from rigid plastic with two skins separated by a layer of expanded foam; they are available in different sizes with hinged doors or removable lids. Usually known as a *cool (or cold) box*, they work equally well at keeping hot food hot. Although quite light to carry they are rather bulky and loaded with food could really only be used for travelling when using a car, caravan, boat or public transport.

Not all cool boxes are sold with an *ice pack*, so make sure you buy at least one, but the more the better, to use in the box. Keep the ice pack in the freezer part of the fridge so that it is ready at a moment's notice for a spur-of-the-moment picnic.

Insulated bags are also invaluable for cold food. They are easier to carry than cool boxes and some people find them better for packing into a car or a haversack. Some have the advantage of packing flat when not in use, which is convenient when travelling food is needed on an outward journey only.

The most luxurious cool box is the kind that plugs into a car battery so that you have all the advantages of a *portable fridge*. If you travel with food in your car a great deal, or plan to drive to Turkey or India, it might be worth investing in such a piece of travelling food equipment. With restaurant food and drink so expensive it wouldn't take long to recover the cost, especially if there are a lot of you.

212

To keep just part of a meal really cold, like ice-cream or salad, a wide-necked *insulated food container* is indispensable. A vacuum flask will keep food chilled for up to 6 hours, and frozen up to 4 hours. It is essential to chill the flask first for 15–30 minutes with ice-cubes, then tip them out and if possible dry inside the flask. Pack the food straight into the container or put in separate portions of food surrounded by more ice-cubes.

I like to carry an insulated container full of ice cubes and some of the insulated ice buckets travel quite well, however hot the weather. The ice can be used for adding to drinks or when melted for rinsing glasses or dishes. One family I know will never venture far in summer without their soda-water machine, drinking water, cordials and ice. If you travel with lots of children addicted to carbonated drinks such a plan might save you a fortune at holiday drinks stands.

Freezer-centre bags made from bonded brown paper are also useful for transporting your own prepared food.

Instead of buying an insulated box it is quite easy to make your own. Start with a really strong cardboard or wooden box. Stick a good layer (1–2 in/2.5–5 cm) of foam plastic over the inside surfaces. Make a padded lid to fit the top and attach handles for carrying. Remember to pack everything in a large plastic bag before storing in the box to contain any spillages. If you can, chill the food thoroughly before packing it and some foods can be lightly frozen first to ensure they arrive at their destination in tip-top condition. And food that needs to be kept cool but not chilled, like a salad, is often best packed in a lidded plastic container with the dressing in a screw-topped jar firmly wedged amongst the salad so that it can be poured over just before serving.

Finally, after taking trouble to pack your food so that it stays cold, try to keep the container in the shade as much as possible, not in the back window of the car, for instance. A rug or cushion laid over the container will help insulate it further.

A great deal of the advice for cold food applies equally well to hot food because once again we are interested in keeping the food as near its original temperature as possible, which means insulating it from the surrounding air. A cool box could also be described as a *hot box*. Instead of the ice pack, I wrap a hot brick (not so hot that it burns — warm it through in the oven) in tea towels and pack it beside hot jacket potatoes or an apple pie. But remember that plastic can melt if exposed to high temperatures so take care.

Some years ago we made a *hay box* which we have found very useful ever since — not least during power cuts in severe weather. Any strong wooden, metal or cardboard box can be used. Simply fold cloth or paper into the base and sides of the box; use clothes pegs or Sellotape to hold in place. Spread fresh but dry hay (the smell alone gives you an appetite) over the base, put in the piping hot food and cover with plenty of hay and a cloth. Replace the lid and leave undisturbed until needed. You will be amazed at how the heat is maintained. This method of slow-cooking has been used in the country for centuries as a way of saving heat.

Hot soups, casseroled dishes and even hot rice keep perfectly for some hours in vacuum and other insulated containers. The wide-necked kind are the easiest to use for this sort of food.

Now that the Take-Away food shop is such a common sight in our High Streets, many people are more familiar with how well hot food travels. I sometimes use the same kind of *aluminium food containers* with cardboard or foil lids for transporting hot food. Make sure that the container and its contents are really heated through in an oven before wrapping in cloth or paper and storing in an insulated bag or box.

The latest vacuum flasks have a siphon action which is excellent for using while actually moving or for older people or children whose grip may be unsteady. However I would advise using the *siphon flask* for hot water or black coffee only because it may be difficult to clean the siphon after pouring soup or milk.

A picnic basket or hamper is also an asset if you can happen on one cheaply. My parents use a marvellous fully-fitted one complete with all the dishes and cutlery needed for 8 people. I have lined a lidded Somerset willow basket with fabric to make an easy-to-carry container for food or utensils. The large handle over the top allows the basket to be carried upright, which does make for less spillage. But any strong carrying box or basket can be used.

Recently I have seen some plastic picnic sets which pack neatly into an oval carrier and some of the insulated bags and boxes now come fully equipped. There are picnic sets sold that are a series of plastic trays with divisions for different foods similar to air flight food trays. Filled with food, the trays nest together with a lid to make transporting them easier. I can see that these could be very useful for eating from *en route* but think that the design could restrict one's choice of food.

Since the derestriction of the price of school meals the number of pupils taking their own school lunch has risen dramatically. And now we are seeing some new ideas for *lunch boxes*. Some of these feature almost unbreakable, leakproof flasks and similar plates and cutlery which are excellent for children. There is nothing more dispiriting than discovering your sandwiches sodden with orange juice. When buying packed lunch equipment for older children and adults check that it will fit easily into a satchel or briefcase.

It can also be fun and cheap to make your own travelling food carrier. Try adapting an old suitcase or kitbag by using sticky backed plastic to line the container and decorating the outside. Children enjoy painting an old lidded biscuit tin or plastic box to use as a lunch box; with a firmly attached handle they are more difficult to lose amongst the other lunch boxes at school.

If you are a serious picnicker I'm sure you will consider a *picnic stove* essential. Just lighting one makes me feel jolly. There are three main types. The smallest is the solid fuel burner which uses metaldehyde to provide heat. This kind is suitable for boiling a kettle or heating some soup but not much more. The running cost is quite high but the equipment is very compact and is therefore excellent for packing into a haversack for a walking trip.

Paraffin stoves of the Primus type are available from camping shops but these are rather messy for picnics and I always lose the pricker! But I'm sure a Primus supporters' club must exist and no doubt one can learn to love these stoves eventually.

I prefer the small gas burner that runs on butane gas. Propane gas is rather bulky and heavy to carry around but if you always picnic in a Land-Rover that may suit you. Camping Gaz is now so widely available that I prefer to use it and the burner is very neat and adjustable. It is suitable for cooking all picnic food and the light fitment for this gas is useful for evening picnics.

For holidays and day-long picnics it's fun to pack a *barbecue set*. One of the small Hibachi types is easily portable complete with charcoal and barbecue firelighters.

I am very happy to sit on the ground on a *rug* but for those who much prefer to sit at a table to eat, like most French picnickers, there are some marvellously neat *picnic sets*. The chairs and stools fit into the table and everything folds up to the size of a briefcase.

216

To be able to prepare travelling food at short notice (and because we live in the country) I depend upon a well-stocked store cupboard and freezer. After all, when we do have good weather in Britain one wants to take advantage of it quickly. And if you have school children how often one is told as they are going to bed that they need a packed lunch in the morning because of a class nature trail!

Because there is nothing more annoying than forgetting an essential piece of equipment, here is a checklist for travelling food for you to tick as a safeguard before setting off. Not every item is needed each time but it's what we've put together over the years for coping with all situations and any number of people. I keep a pared down version wrapped in a picnic rug in the boot of the car for instant travelling meals.

CHECKLIST OF TRAVELLING FOOD EQUIPMENT
Basket, hamper or container for equipment
Cool box or food container and 1 or 2 ice packs
Hay box for hot food
Vacuum flasks for liquids: 1 siphon, 1 jug
Wide-necked insulated flask for hot or cold food
Set of plates in 2 sizes, plastic or earthenware
Set of bowls
Set of glasses (plastic for children)
Set of mugs or cups, suitable for soup and beverages
Cutlery to accompany crockery
Set of wooden platters and baskets for serving food
Can opener, corkscrew and bottle opener
Wine stopper that fits any bottle
Drinking straws (useful for cars and boats)
Serrated knife for cutting bread, meat, fruit, etc.
Screw-topped jars for salad dressing, sugar, salt, etc.
Cloth or paper napkins and tablecloth
Kitchen paper, cling film, aluminium foil

Teacloth
Kettle, tea or coffee pot
Saucepan and frying pan and lids, or a Chinese Wok for stir frying
Collection of lidded plastic boxes in assorted sizes
Picnic stove, gas and matches
Plastic bags for rubbish and twist ties (bin liners or dustbin)
Sponge, bottle of water and small container of detergent
Rug — the best ones have a waterproof layer on one side
Plastic sheet
Drinking water container and/or carrier
Picnic table and chairs, sun umbrella
Barbecue set and charcoal
Baby wipes or other moist tissues for mopping up generally

This list looks enormous but most of it I keep in a cupboard out of the way until needed. But sometimes it's fun to improvise totally and cope with just a knife and a corkscrew!

I hope this book has been helpful to your travelling food ventures and that you have discovered food and advice to enliven your picnics, packed lunches or desktop eating.

If it be true that travel does broaden the mind, let also the palate be delighted while remembering the old proverb, 'Setting out well is a quarter of the journey'.

Index

Aïoli, 107
  les crudités avec l'aïoli, 115
All-Bran fruit loaf, 175
Almond:
  cream flan, 157
  spiced rice salad with raisins, 123
  stuffed peaches, 166
Alphabet soup, 19–20
American burger sandwich, 54–6
Anchovy:
  butter, 60
  pissaladière, 101
  pizza Napoletana, 99
  salade Niçoise, 117
  stuffed eggs, 149
Apple:
  Dorset apple cake, 180
  fresh apple drink, 195
  pie with cheese pastry, 156–7
  rice salad with celery and walnuts, 118–19
Apricot:
  loaf, 40–1
  soup, 30
  squares, 181–2
Artichoke, Jerusalem:
  and olive salad, 120
  soup, 25–6
Asparagus tart, 89
Aubergines:
  ratatouille, 114
Avocado:
  and prawn filling, 50
  guacamole, 75–6
  salad, 116–17

Bacon:
  and celery pizza, 99
  crunchy bacon squares, 187
  and leek salad, 120
  meat loaf ring, 141
  and sweetcorn filling for potatoes, 148
  turkey and thyme pies, 83–4
Banana:
  chocolate cake, 179
  milk, 197
  raisin and cream cheese filling, 53
Barbecue menu, lunch or supper, 210
Basic pizza dough, 96
Beans:
  Boston pork'n'beans, 131
  broad bean salad, 109–10
  chilli con carne, 130
  haricot bean and tuna salad, 119
  minestrone, 23–4
  red kidney bean salad with sweetcorn, 122
  Wurstsuppe, 134–5
Beef:
  American hamburger, 55
  carbonnade flamande, 135
  chilli con carne, 130
  corned beef and celery filling, 52
  Cornish pasties, 79–80
  curry, 136

Frikadeller med Rödkaal, 133–4
Hungarian goulash, 138
meat loaf ring, 141
and mushroom pie, 84–5
potted, Miss Parloa's, 73–4
pressed tongue, 142
shepherd's pies, 139–40
and tomato pasties, 80–1
Beetroot:
  Bortsch, 27
Biscuits and cookies:
  apricot squares, 181–2
  cheese and peanut triangles, 188
  chocolate pineapple squares, 182–3
  crunchy bacon squares, 187
  digestive biscuits, 189
  Grasmere gingerbread, 183
  healthfood flapjack, 184
  oat and raisin cookies, 185–6
  oatcakes, 188–9
  sesame seed biscuits, 186–7
  sultana and marmalade biscuits, 186
  wholewheat cheese shortbread, 190
Blackcurrant milk, 197
Bortsch, 27
Boston pork'n'beans, 131
Bread:
  apricot loaf, 40
  celery and walnut, 44
  herb or garlic loaf, 59
  hot stuffed loaf, 59
  onion herb, 41
  pudding, 161
  three grain, 33
  treacle sultana, 42–3
  walnut, 42
  Welsh teabread, 45
  white, 34
  white milk, 35–6
  white speedy, 36–7
  wholemeal cheese scone ring, 46
  wholemeal fruit, 43
  wholemeal quickest, 37–8
Broad bean salad, 109–10
Butter:
  anchovy, 60
  garlic, 60
  herb, 60
  honey, 61
  maître d'hotel, 60
  mustard, 60
  onion, 60
  tarragon, 60
  to clarify, 72
Butterscotch creams, 165–6

Cabbage:
  Frikadeller med Rödkaal, 133–4
  minestrone, 23–4
  red cabbage salad, 113
  white cabbage salad, 114
  Wurstsuppe, 134–5

Cakes:
  carrot and orange, 178–9
  chocolate banana, 179
  Dorset apple, 180
  Jordan's marmalade, 177–8
  lunchbox, 180–1
  wholemeal chocolate walnut, 176–7
  wholemeal fruit, 175–6
Canadian:
  club sandwich, 56
  cooked salad dressing, 109
  raisin pie, 155–6
Caramel milk, 197
Carbonnade flamande, 135
Caribbean cooler, 195
Carrot:
  creamy carrot soup, 28
  les crudités, 115
  and orange cake, 178–9
  salad, 11
Casserole dishes:
  beef or lamb curry, 136
  Boston pork'n'beans, 136
  carbonnade flamande, 135
  chicken with paprika and cummin, 129
  chilli con car ne, 130
  Hungarian goulash, 138
  lamb chops boulangère, 137
  rabbit with prunes, 131–2
Celery:
  and bacon pizza, 99
  chicken salad with pineapple, 121
  and corned beef sandwich filling, 52
  les crudités, 115
  rice salad with apple and walnut, 118–19
  soup with green pepper, 22
  and walnut loaf, 44–5
Champagne, June, 200
Cheese:
  apple pie with cheese pastry, 156–7
  and bacon sandwich filling, 52
  Cheddar and pepper filling, 52
  Cheshire, potted, 74
  cottage cheese with herbs and garlic, 147–8
  endive and blue cheese salad, 117
  English tartlets, 91–2
  Liptauer, 75
  and peanut triangles, 188
  sesame seed biscuits, 186
  Wensleydale, potted, 74
  wholewheat shortbread, 190
Cheesecake:
  Hungarian, 163–4
  strawberry-topped, 164–5
Chicken:
  liver pâté, 65
  with paprika and cummin, 129
  and pimento pie, 85–6
  salad with celery and pineapple, 121
  potted, 72
  spiced joints, 144
  spiced pasties, 81
Chicory salad with orange, 112
Chilled cucumber soup, 27
Chilli con carne, 130
Chocolate:
  banana cake, 179
  hot marshmallow drink, 201
  milk, 196
  pineapple squares, 182
  rich mousse, 168
  wholewheat walnut cake, 176–7
Cod's roe, taramasalata, 71
Coconut tart, 156
Coffee:
  frozen mousse, 169
  Gaelic coffee, 201
Cornish pasties, 79–80
Courgettes:
  ratatouille, 114
  and green pepper frittata, 151
Cream, soured cream dressing, 108
Cream cheese:
  and banana, raisin sandwich filling, 53
  salad dressing, 108
  spreads, 53
Cream of mushroom soup, 22–3
Creamy carrot soup, 28
Crunchy bacon squares, 187
Cucumber:
  chilled soup, 29
  gazpacho, 28–9
  and salmon sandwich filling, 51
Crudités avec l'aïoli, 115
Curd cheese:
  homemade, 53
  Hungarian cheesecake, 163–4
  Russian pashka, 161–2
  spreads, 53
  strawberry-topped cheesecake, 164–5

Dhal soup, 20
Digestive biscuits, 189
Dorset apple cake, 180
Dressings:
  Canadian cooked salad, 109
  cream cheese, 108
  French, 105
  soured cream, 108
  yoghurt and lemon, 107
Dried fruit:
  All-Bran fruit loaf, 43–4
  bread pudding, 161
  date and nut sandwich filling, 49
  lunchbox cake, 180–1
  and nut salad, 124–5
  rabbit with prunes, 131–2
  Welsh tea-bread, 45
  wholemeal fruit cake, 175–6
  wholemeal fruit loaf, 43–4
Duck terrine with orange, 67

Eggs:
  anchovy stuffed, 149
  and chive sandwich filling, 49
  courgette and green pepper frittata, 151
  curried sandwich filling, 49
  devilled stuffed, 148–9
  mushroom omelette, 150
  salade Niçoise, 117
  and sausage pie, 86–7
  Spanish onion tortilla, 150
  spinach pancake, 152
  tomato and herb stuffed, 149

Endive and blue cheese salad, 117
English cheese tartlets, 91–2
Equipment for travelling food: 211ff,
  checklist, 217
Equivalence tables, 13

Fillings for sandwiches and rolls, 49–53
Fish:
  smoked fish plait, 87–8
  smoked salmon quiche, 89
  see also tuna fish
Flapjack, healthfood, 184
French dressing, 105
French sandwich, 57–8
Fresh apple drink, 195
Fresh apricot soup, 30
Fresh lemon tarts, 159
Frikadeller med Rödkaal, 133–4
Frittata, courgette and green pepper, 151
Frozen coffee mouse, 169
Fruit:
  based drinks, 193–5
  flavoured milk, 197
  punch, 198
  tartlets, 160

Gaelic coffee, 201
Game pie, 95–6
Garlic:
  aïoli, 107
  cottage cheese with herbs, 147–8
  les crudités avec l'aïoli, 115
Gazpacho, 28–9
German onion tart, 90–1
Gingerbread, Grasmere, 183–4
Glazed baked ham, 143
Granary rolls, 38–9
Grape-juice cocktail, 199
Grasmere gingerbread, 183–4
Green lentil salad with cervalat, 122–3
Green salad, 112–13
Guacamole, 75–6

Ham:
  glazed baked, 143
  and red pepper pizza, 100
  smoked ham and pasta salad, 124
  spiced and tomato filling, 52
  and veal pie, 94–5
Hamburger, 55
Haricot bean and tuna salad, 119
Healthfood flapjack, 184
Herbs:
  cottage cheese with garlic, 147–8
  hot herb loaf, 59
  and tomato stuffed eggs, 149
Homemade yoghurt, 170–1
Hot:
  drinks, 200–1
  marshmallow chocolate, 201
  stuffed loaf, 59
Household stock, 19
Hungarian:
  cheesecake, 163–4
  goulash, 138

Ice-cream:
  coffee mousse, 169

  strawberry, 169–70
Ice cubes, zesty, 193

Jacket potatoes, 146–7
Jerusalem artichoke:
  and olive salad, 120
  soup, 25–6
Jordan's marmalade cake, 177–8
June champagne, 200

Kebabs of pork, 145
Kidney:
  soup, 28
  in wine sauce, 147
Kipper pâté, 70

Lamb:
  chops boulangère, 137–8
  chops en papillote, 140–1
  curry, 136
  kidneys in wine sauce, 147
Layered sandwich loaf, 58
Leek salad with bacon, 120
Lemon:
  barley water, 198–9
  fresh lemon tarts, 159
  liquidiser lemonade, 194
  and yoghurt dressing, 107
Lentils:
  dhal soup, 20
  green lentil salad with cervalat, 122–3
Liptauer cheese, 75
Liquidiser lemonade, 194
Liver sausage sandwich fillings, 51
Loaf:
  All-Bran fruit, 175
  apricot, 40–1
  celery and walnut, 44–5
  crown, 35
  herb and garlic, 59
  hot stuffed, 59
  layered sandwich, 58
  plaited, 35
  wholemeal fruit, 43–4
Lunchbox:
  cake, 180–1
  menus, 205

Marmalade:
  Jordan's cake, 177–8
  and sultana biscuits, 186
Mayonnaise, 106
Meat loaf ring, 141
Menus, 205ff
Milk:
  banana, 197
  blackcurrant, 197
  caramel, 197
  chocolate, 196
  fruit flavoured, 197
  shopper's life-line, 199
Minestrone, 23–4
Minced beef:
  Frikadeller med Rödkaal, 133–4
  hamburger, 55
  meat loaf ring, 141

shepherd's pies, 139–40
and tomato pasties, 80–1
Miss Parloa's potted beef, 73–4
Mousse:
chocolate, 168
frozen coffee, 169
raspberry, 167–8
Mushroom:
and beef pie, 84–5
les crudités, 115
à la grecque, 116
omelette, 150
pizza, 100
sandwich filling, 51
soup, cream of, 22–3

Nuts:
and dried fruit salad, 124–5
coconut tart, 158
crunchy nut yoghurt topping, 171
date and nut sandwich filling, 49
peanut butter with raisins, 50
spiced rice salad with almonds and raisins, 123
see also almonds, walnuts

Oats:
healthfood flapjack, 184
oatcakes, 188–9
and raisin cookies, 185–6
three grain bread, 33
Omelettes:
mushroom, 150
spinach, 152
see also frittata, tortilla and pancake
Onion:
butter, 60
German tart, 90–1
and herb bread, 41
lamb chops boulangère, 137–8
Spanish onion tortilla, 150
Orange:
and carrot cake, 178–9
Jordan's marmalade cake, 177
quick jellies, 166
quick orange or grapefruit squash, 193

Packed lunches, 204–6
Pancake spinach, 152
Pasta and smoked ham salad, 124
Pasties:
Cornish, 79–80
minced beef and tomato, 80–1
spiced chicken, 81
Tiddy oggy, 82
Pastry:
hot water crust, 93
rich shortcrust, 88
shortcrust, 79
tartlet, 160
Pâté:
kipper, 70
quick chicken liver, 65
taramasalata, 71
tuna fish, 70
Peaches:
fresh apricot soup, 30

stuffed, 166–7
Peanuts:
butter with raisins, 50
and cheese triangles, 188
Perfect boiled rice, 136
Picnic:
all-weather menu, 210
summer menu, 207
Picnic parcels, 140–1
Pies:
apple with cheese pastry, 156–7
beef and mushroom, 84
Canadian raisin, 155–6
chicken and pimento, 85
game, 95–6
sausage and egg, 86
smoked fish plait, 87
traditional pork, 92–4
turkey, thyme and bacon, 83
veal and ham, 94–5
Pineapple:
chicken salad with celery, 121
pinepricot juice, 195
tuna fish sandwich filling, 195
Pinepricot juice, 195
Pissaladière, 101
Pizza:
bacon and celery, 99
basic dough, 97–8
ham and red pepper, 100
mushroom, 100
Napoletana, 99
speedy dough, 97–8
tomato sauce, 98
tuna with capers, 101–2
Plum clafoutis, 162
Poppy seed rolls, 39–40
Pork:
Boston pork'n'beans, 131
Frikadeller med Rödkaal, 133–4
kebabs, 145
meat loaf ring, 141
rillettes, 65
traditional pork pie, Melton Mowbray, 92–4
Potato:
jacket potatoes and fillings, 146–8
lamb chops boulangère, 137–8
lamb chops en papillote, 140
scalloped, 132
shepherd's pies, 139–40
Wilma's salad, 121
Potted:
beef, Miss Parloa's, 73–4
cheese, Cheshire, 74
Wensleydale, 74
chicken or turkey, 72–3
prawns, 72
Prawns:
and avocado salad, 116–17
and avocado sandwich filling, 50
potted, 72
smoked fish plait, 87
Prepared meals menu, 208
Pressed ox tongue, 142
Punch, fruit, 198

Quatre épices, 64

Quiche:
  asparagus, 89
  Lorraine, 88–9
  smoked salmon, 89
Quick:
  chicken liver pâté, 65
  orange jellies, 166
  orange (or grapefruit) squash, 193
Quickest wholemeal bread, 37–8

Rabbit:
  with prunes, 131–2
  terrine, 68
Raisins:
  Canadian pie, 155–6
  dried fruit and nut, 124
  oat cookies, 185–6
  with peanut butter, 50
  Russian pashka, 161
  spiced rice salad with almonds, 123
  treacle girdle scones, 184
Raspberry mousses, 167–8
Ratatouille, 114–15
Red cabbage salad, 113
Red kidney bean salad with sweetcorn, 122
Rice:
  boiled rice, 136–7
  salad with celery, apple and walnuts, 118
  spiced salad with almonds and raisins, 123
Rich chocolate mousses, 168
Rillettes, 65–6
Rolls:
  burger, 56
  granary, 38–9
  poppy seed, 39–40
Russian pashka, 161–2

Salad:
  avocado and prawn, 116–17
  broad bean, 109–10
  carrot, 111
  chicken with celery and pineapple, 121
  chicory with orange, 112
  les crudités avec l'aïoli, 115
  dried fruit and nut, 124–5
  endive and blue cheese, 117
  green, 112
  green lentil with cervalat, 122–3
  haricot bean and tuna, 119
  Jerusalem artichoke and olive, 120
  leek with bacon, 120
  mushrooms à la grecque, 116
  Niçoise, 117–18
  ratatouille, 114–15
  red cabbage, 113
  red kidney bean with sweetcorn, 122
  rice with celery, apple and walnuts, 118–19
  smoked ham and pasta, 124
  spiced rice with almonds and raisins, 123
  spinach, 111
  tomato, 110
  Wilma's potato, 121
  white cabbage, 114

Sandwich:
  American burger, 54–6
  Canadian club, 56

French, 57–8
fillings, 49–53
layered loaf, 58
pan bagna, 57
Poor Boy, 58
Scandinavian open, 57
toasted, 54
Sandwich fillings:
  l'aillade à la toulousaine, 50
  bacon and cheese, 52
  banana and raisin, 53
  Cheddar cheese and pepper, 52
  corned beef and celery, 52
  curried egg, 49
  date and nut, 49
  egg and chive, 49
  liver sausage, sweetcorn and pimento, 51
  mushroom, 51
  peanut butter with raisins, 50
  prawn and avocado, 50
  salmon and cucumber, 51
  sardine and watercress, 50
  spiced ham and tomato, 52
  spiced liver sausage, 51
  tuna fish with pineapple, 52
Sardine and watercress filling, 50
Sausage:
  bratwurst, Mettwurst, and Frankfurters in
    Wurstsuppe, 134–5
  and egg pie, 86–7
  green lentil salad with cervalat, 122–3
  liver sausage fillings, 51
  smoked ham and pasta salad, 124
Sauce:
  l'aïoli, 107
  kidneys in wine, 147
  mayonnaise, 106
  sultanas in sherry, 172
  vinaigrette, 105
Scandinavian open sandwiches, 57
Scones:
  treacle girdle scones, 184–5
  wholemeal cheese scone round, 46
Seasoned butters, 60–1
Sesame seed:
  biscuits, 186–7
  burger rolls, 56
Shopper's lifeline, 199
Small:
  raspberry mousses, 167–8
  shepherd's pies, 139–40
Smoked:
  fish plait, 87–8
  ham and pasta salad, 124
  salmon quiche, 89
Soups:
  alphabet, 19–20
  apricot, 30
  artichoke, 25–6
  bortsch, 27
  celery and green pepper, 22
  creamy carrot, 28
  cucumber, chilled, 29
  dhal, 20
  gazpacho, 28–9
  kidney, 26
  minestrone, 23–4

mushroom, cream of, 22–3
spinach, 24–5
tomato, 21
Wurstsuppe, 134–5
Soured cream dressing, 108
Speedy:
pizza dough, 97–8
white bread, 36–7
Spices:
beef or lamb curry, 136
chicken joints, 144
chicken with paprika and cummin, 129
chicken pasties, 81
Grasmere gingerbread, 183
liver sausage, 51
rice salad with almonds and raisins, 123
quatre épices, 64
Spinach:
pancake, 152
salad, 111
soup, 24–5
Tuscan tart, 90
Strawberry:
ice-cream, 169–70
topped cheesecake, 164–5
Stuffed:
eggs, 148–9
peaches, 166–7
Sultana:
and marmalade biscuits, 186
in sherry, 172
treacle bread, 42–3
Sweetcorn:
and bacon hot filling for potatoes, 149
liver sausage and pimento sandwich filling,
51
and red kidney bean salad, 122

Tarts:
almond cream flan, 157
asparagus, 89
coconut, 158
English cheese, 91–2
fresh lemon, 159
fruit tartlets, 160
German onion, 90–1
Tuscan spinach, 90
Taramasalata, 71
Terrine:
duck with orange, 67
rabbit, 68
turkey liver, 69
Three grain bread, 33
Tiddy oggy, 82
Toasted sandwiches, 54
Tomato:
and herb stuffed eggs, 149
juice, 194
minced beef pasties, 80
pizza sauce, 98

ratatouille, 114
salad, 110
soup, 21
and spiced ham filling, 52
Tongue, pressed ox, 142
Tortilla, Spanish onion, 150
Traditional pork pie, 92–4
Treacle:
sultana bread, 42–3
girdle scones, 184–5
Tuna fish:
with capers pizza, 101
and haricot bean salad, 119
pâté, 70–1
and pineapple sandwich filling, 50
Turkey:
liver terrine, 69
potted, 72
and thyme and bacon pies, 83–4
Tuscan spinach tart, 90

Veal and ham pie, 94–5

Walnut:
l'aillade à la toulousaine, 50
bread, 42
and celery loaf, 44–5
rice salad with celery and apple, 118–19
wholemeal chocolate cake, 176–7
Welsh tea-bread, 45
White:
bread, 34
cabbage salad, 114
milk bread, 35–6
speedy bread, 36–7
Wholemeal:
cheese scone round, 46
cheese shortbread, 190
chocolate walnut cake, 176–7
digestive biscuits, 189
fruit cake, 175–6
fruit loaf, 43–4
quickest bread, 37
Wholewheat cheese shortbread, 190
Wilma's potato salad, 121
Wine:
curaçao in Caribbean cooler, 195
in fruit punch, 198
kidneys in wine sauce, 147
sultanas in sherry, 172
vermouth in pinepricot juice, 195
Wurstsuppe, 134–5

Yoghurt:
homemade, 170–1
and lemon dressing, 107
toppings, 171–2

Zesty ice cubes, 193–4